OPERATION TIMBER:
PAGES FROM THE
SAVIMBI DOSSIER

Edited with an Introduction
by
William Minter

Africa World Press, Inc.

P.O. Box 1892
Trenton, New Jersey 08607
(609) 695-3766

Africa World Press, Inc.
P.O. Box 1892
Trenton, NJ 08607

First Printing 1988

Cover Design by Ife Nii-Owoo

Typeset by TypeHouse of Pennington, Inc.

Library of Congress Catalog Card Number: 88-71419

ISBN: 0-86543-103-5   Cloth
       0-86543-104-3   Paper

CONTENTS

ANGOLA

CONGO

ZAIRE

Cabinda

CABINDA

ZAIRE

UIGE

Luanda

LUANDA

KWANZA NORTE

MALANJE

LUNDA NORTE

BENGO

KWANZA SUL

LUNDA SUL

Luau

Benguela Railroad

Benguela

Kuito

Cuemba

Munhango

BENGUELA

HUAMBO

BIE

MOXICO

Cangamba

Mocamedes Railroad

HUILA

Menongue

Cuando River

ZAMBIA

Namibe

Lubango

Cuito Cuanavale

Lomba River

NAMIBE

CUNENE

Mavinga

KUANDO KUBANGO

Jamba

NAMIBIA

BOTSWANA

Africa News map/Becky Kohler

IV

ACKNOWLEDGEMENTS

For making possible access to the documents cited in *História de uma Traição* and for facilitating work on this book, I am grateful to Manuel Pedro Pacavira, Ambassador of the People's Republic of Angola to the United Nations, to Raimundo Sotto-Maior, former director of the Angolan news agency (ANGOP), and to the staff of the information department of the MPLA Workers Party. David Martin and Phyllis Johnson, of the Southern African Research and Documentation Centre (SARDC) in Harare, kindly made available notes from their interviews with Portuguese officers.

The initial translation of the documents from *Expresso* was done by Stephanos Stephanides. I am responsible for the final version of that translation, and for the translations of other documents and sources cited. I have opted for a close-to-literal translation in order to convey a sense of the originals. I am also responsible, of course, for any errors of fact or judgement in the introduction and footnotes.

Whenever possible, I have identified place names in the footnotes, using Patricia K. Thompson and Carl R. Page, *Gazeteer of Angola* (Washington, Defense Mapping Agency, 1986), as well as the Michelin map of Central and South Africa and the map of Angola published by the Main Administration of Geodesy and Cartography (Moscow, 1986). Spellings of place names have been left as in the original documents.

William Minter
Washington, DC
March, 1988

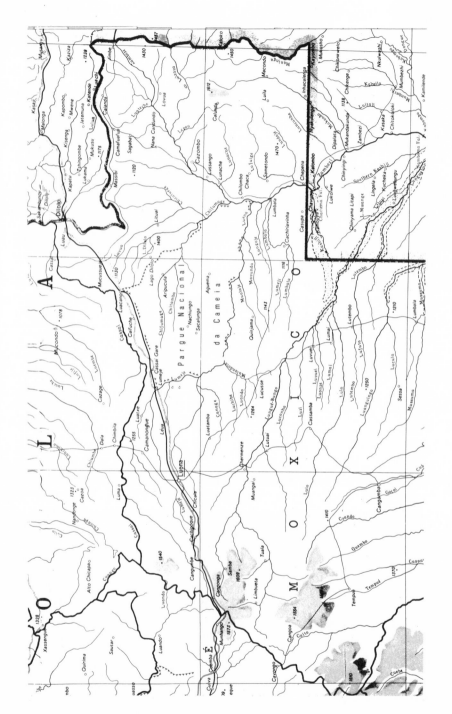

VI

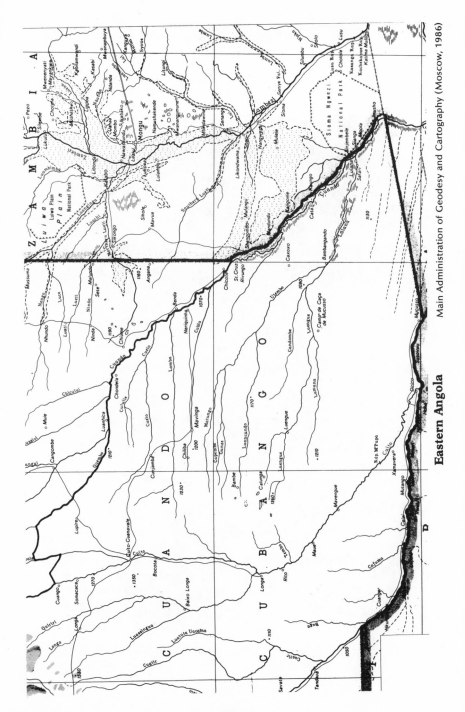

Eastern Angola

Main Administration of Geodesy and Cartography (Moscow, 1986)

VII

Col. Oliver North and Jonas Savimbi with John M. Fisher, Chairman of the private American Security Council. (Photo taken from ASC Newsletter)

PREFACE

All too often, U.S. policy towards Africa has been driven by the twin demons of racism and ignorance. The whole world has for decades condemned the apartheid South African regime. But it took years of protests, demonstrations and parliamentary maneuvers before the full U.S. Congress passed limited sanctions against South Africa, in the form of the Comprehensive Anti-Apartheid Act of 1986. Even this moderate step had to overcome a Presidential veto. The Reagan administration is still reluctant to enforce it vigorously.

As South Africa escalates its internal repression of those who seek democracy and justice, it is imperative to renew efforts to isolate that regime. We must impose comprehensive sanctions to deprive Pretoria's rulers of the resources they use to enforce poverty for the many and privilege for the few. It is also urgent to expose and counter South Africa's war against neighboring African states, with its enormous toll of death and destruction.

South Africa's war in Angola is cloaked in a particularly dense cloud of ignorance and disinformation. It is subsidized by U.S. 'covert' aid to South Africa's racist army in that country, through the UNITA movement headed by Jonas Savimbi. Many who claim to oppose apartheid excuse this aid to Savimbi, beguiled by his presentation of the war as an anti-communist crusade against the Cuban troops aiding the Angolan government. Savimbi downplays the aid he gets from South Africa, and the press generally obscures the real picture: South African troops fighting side-by-side with UNITA in battles for which Savimbi claims credit and the

South African-supplied landmines which UNITA plants in the fields of Angolan peasants. South Africa's powerful G-5 long-range artillery and U.S.-supplied Stinger missiles, co-ordinated by South African generals, are used together against an independent African country.

Savimbi is a charismatic figure who impresses Western journalists and conservative politicians. But his credentials as a nationalist leader are fatally discredited by over a decade of close collaboration with South Africa. The collection of documents in this book, published for the first time in the English language, also reveal that even his earlier history has its secret scandal: a covert military alliance with the Portuguese colonial army he claimed to be fighting.

These documents are edited and introduced by William Minter, a long-time scholar of southern Africa. His book *Portuguese Africa and the West* (1971) exposed U.S. ties with the Portuguese war against African independence. His most recent book— *King Solomon's Mines Revisited: Western Interests and the Burdened History of Southern Africa* (1986) — has been widely and favorably reviewed. He has investigated these documents, which some UNITA supporters have claimed as forgeries, and discovered substantial evidence for their authenticity.

The result is historical documentation with direct relevance for U.S. policy. The European powers subdued Africa with the aid of 'divide-and-conquer' strategies. The apartheid regime and its defenders are relying on similar strategies today. If the U.S. is to support democracy and combat racism in southern Africa, and at home, we need to expose such covert maneuvers to the light of day. For that we need reliable information, such as the documentation in this book. I urge all those concerned with the struggle against apartheid to read it.

Representative Mervyn Dymally
House of Representatives
Washington, DC

March, 1988

INTRODUCTION

"Can This Man Save Africa?" read the headline of a May 1987 *Reader's Digest* profile of Jonas Savimbi. The "charismatic, swashbuckling general has stopped Soviet imperialism dead in its tracks in Angola," the article continued, and he "may herald a democratic upsurge in black Africa."

Even *Reader's Digest* admitted, toward the end of the article, that Savimbi enjoys a military alliance with South Africa. For the magazine, however, as for many U.S. policymakers, this alliance does little to tarnish Savimbi's "democratic" image. Even before his $600,000 public relations blitz of Washington in January 1986, Savimbi and publicists for his National Union for the Total Independence of Angola (UNITA) were successfully playing on U.S. Cold War myths and ignorance of southern Africa.

Some critics caution against U.S. aid to UNITA, on the basis of the damage to U.S. foreign policy caused by involvement in South Africa's regional wars. But even such critics often credit Savimbi as a genuine African nationalist, with legitimate claims to a share of power in Angola.

In fact, few outside Angola know much about Savimbi other than the version he himself presents. In part attributable to political bias, this ignorance is also due to a language barrier. Over the years Savimbi's personality—and his skill in English—have impressed many influential journalists, most of whom failed to consult the wider more informative range of sources in Portuguese. Fred Bridgland's recent detailed biography, for example, depends almost entirely on the author's interviews with Savimbi and cites virtually no Portuguese-language sources.

Even in Portuguese the written material available for a more careful judgment is sketchy. The gaps in the history of the Angolan conflict are larger than the patches of reliable information or systematic analysis. This is true for the pre-1975 war against Portuguese colonialism, and even more so for the complex postindependence strife. The numerous studies of international intervention during the period 1974-1976 more often than not simply recycle the same news items from different political perspectives, rarely revealing new information.

Ironically, one of the best documented episodes is still virtually unknown to English-speaking readers. And it is one with a direct relevance to Savimbi's claims to nationalist credentials. A series of documents—a few published in French in 1974, the majority later in Portuguese in Lisbon and Luanda—show that during the last years of the colonial conflict, Savimbi maintained a formal agreement for military collaboration with the Portuguese colonial troops he was supposedly fighting. Under "Operation Timber," as it was codenamed by the Portuguese military authorities, the two combined their forces against the guerrillas of the Popular Movement for the Liberation of Angola (MPLA), the movement that is now the ruling party in independent Angola.

The documentation for Operation Timber—which Savimbi denounced as forgeries—is not complete. And its significance for the present debate varies with the perspective of each debater. For many of Savimbi's overseas supporters, a record of collaboration with colonialism is a matter of indifference or even of praise. Others, however, may find in this material reason to doubt Savimbi's commitment to African freedom or at least his honesty. Whatever one's view of the events, the evidence is sufficient to establish this episode as part of the historical record. The full Savimbi dossier is not yet available, much less a comprehensive history of Angola in the last quarter-century, but the present collection is one that no one concerned with Angola can ignore.

The following introduction summarizes the historical background of Operation Timber and presents the evidence available for the operation itself as well as a brief overview of events following Angola's independence. A guide to sources appears as Appendix 1; Appendix 2 contains several additional testimonies on UNITA previously unavailable in English.

The Road to Luso:
Portuguese Colonialism and the Anticolonial War

Before 1961, when a wave of violence announced to the world the Angolan anticolonial struggle, Portugal's African colonies were seen as tranquil backwaters in a continent of nationalist awakening. Gilberto Freyre, a Brazilian anthropologist who visited Angola and Mozambique in the 1950s, had popularized his thesis of "lusotropicalism," claiming a special capacity of the Portuguese for relating to "tropical" dark-skinned peoples. In contrast to the rigid racial separation congenial to northern Europeans, he argued, miscegenation in Brazil and in Portuguese Africa pointed to a capacity for racial and cultural assimilation.

The right-wing dictatorship of António Salazar, established in Portugal since 1928, welcomed this Brazilian gloss on its colonial presence. Stress on Portugal's imperial glory, past and present, was an essential element of Salazar's fascist ideology. Financial stability and political repression at home were matched by appeals to develop the resources of "overseas Portugal." Angola, Mozambique, and the smaller Portuguese territories strung from Cape Verde in the Atlantic to Macao on the China coast were not colonies at all, the theory went, but the legacy of a multicontinental Portuguese nation. Other European powers like Britain and France might have more territory and more capital; but Portugal's five centuries of experience, combined with central administration and protectionist policies, could create an exemplary "Portuguese space."

Examined closely, the reality diverged sharply from the grandiose theory. Portuguese ships had indeed touched the coast of what are now Zaire (Congo) and Angola before the year 1500. In the sixteenth century, Portuguese missionaries and traders had persuaded King Afonso of the Kongo, whose territory extended into present-day northern Angola, to convert to Catholicism and had established a presence in his kingdom. Angola's capital, Luanda, founded in 1605, is one of sub-Saharan Africa's oldest cities. Except for seven years of Dutch occupation in the mid-seventeenth century, Luanda was held by Portugal until 1975. To speak of five (or four) centuries of Portuguese *rule*, however—much less of peaceful integration into the Portuguese nation—seriously distorts the historical record.

Until the last quarter of the 19th century, when Portugal along with other European powers completed the division of Africa into the territories we know today, Portuguese rule in Angola was confined to a handful of coastal settlements. Control extended not much more than 150 miles inland from Luanda, along a strip to the north of the Kwanza river, and even less in the hinterland of Benguela, the other major settlement.

Angola's European population in 1846, according to a contemporary survey by Lopes de Lima, numbered only 1,830, with 1,600 of them in Luanda, 39 in Benguela, and 20 in the newly-founded far southern port of Moçamedes.[1] De Lima also counted, in areas under Portuguese control, some 6,000 mestiços (people of mixed race) and 386,000 blacks (86,000 of them classified as slaves). This enclave, encompassing perhaps 10% of Angola's population, was still living off the slave trade to Brazil despite the official abolition of that trade ten years earlier. After Brazil closed its ports to slave traders in 1850, the Portuguese in Angola turned to trading beeswax, ivory, and later rubber.

For Angolans, the early centuries of Portuguese presence were dominated by the slave trade. The export of as many as 20,000 slaves per year across the Atlantic continued into the mid-nineteenth century. The traffic in "indentured laborers"— slaves in all but name—to the Portuguese-owned island of

São Tomé extended well into the twentieth century. As Portugal occupied the Angolan interior, in a series of conquests completed only after World War I, a formal system of forced labor replaced slavery. Although not assigned permanently to "owners," Angolans were nevertheless legally required (and mobilized by force) to provide labor for roadbuilding, plantations and other Portuguese enterprises.

Sugar and later coffee plantations were controlled in large part by Portuguese settlers. For larger enterprises, however, Angola depended on non-Portuguese capital. The Benguela Railway, designed to transport copper from the mines of northern Rhodesia (Zambia) and the Belgian Congo (Zaire), was controlled by Belgian and British capital. The diamond mines of northeastern Angola brought in South African capital as well.

With a smaller capacity than other colonial regimes for mobilizing African labor by means of economic incentives, the Portuguese administration depended to an unusual extent on direct force and brutality. And when, with expansion of coffee production after World War II, a measure of "development" did come to the colony, it was accompanied by a new influx of white settlers. The white population of Angola almost quadrupled from 44,000 in 1940 to 173,000 in 1960. In the coffee-growing region of northern Angola, immigrants using cheap forced labor appropriated African farmland. In the cities whites from Portugal displaced Africans, mestiços and even locally-born whites from urban jobs in the administration and in the private sector.

Faced with the Portuguese police state, nationalist opposition was of necessity underground or from exile. In 1956 the Popular Movement for the Liberation of Angola (MPLA) was founded in Luanda. In the Belgian Congo, Holden Roberto started the Union of the Peoples of Angola (UPA, initially called the Union of Peoples of Northern Angola) in 1957. In June 1960, as the Congo was achieving its tumultuous independence, Portuguese police arrested Dr. Agostinho Neto, an African medical doctor who was to become independent Angola's first president. When some thousand villagers gathered to protest in Catete, some 60 miles outside of

Luanda near Neto's birthplace, soldiers opened fire, killing 30 and wounding about 200. Unlike the parallel massacre in Sharpeville, South Africa, three months earlier, the events in Catete were not reported in the press.

The next year, 1961, Angolans' accumulated grievances finally burst to the surface. On February 4 several hundred MPLA supporters attached a Luanda prison, seeking to release political prisoners they feared would be executed. Seven Portuguese police were killed, but the prisoners were not freed. In the following week police and vigilantes killed hundreds of Africans in the Luanda slums in retaliation.

In March a separate revolt in the north, loosely linked to Roberto's UPA, killed hundreds of Portuguese settlers, removing Portuguese authority for some months. The colonial response was even more brutal. Targetting not only the guerrilla-controlled zones but also suspect Africans elsewhere in the country—i.e., almost any African who had achieved some degree of education—the colonial authorities reimposed order. By mid-year as many as 20,000 Angolans had been killed by colonial troops, militia, or white lynch mobs.

It was in this atmosphere of violence and counterviolence that Angolan exiles had to plan for a prolonged struggle against Portuguese rule. Unlike Britain or Belgium, Portugal was not shocked by the signs of discontent into charting a course towards independence. Both the MPLA and UPA campaigned for African and international support for Angolan independence. Among Portugal's allies in the North Atlantic Treaty Organization (NATO), the Kennedy administration in particular moved briefly to open criticism of Portugal. But the pressure was halting and inconsistent, blocking neither the arms nor the economic support Portugal needed to reimpose control.

Divisions also weakened the nationalist cause. In the March revolt UPA had not only targetted Portuguese civilians— a tactic repudiated by the MPLA—but its supporters had also slaughtered educated Angolans (*assimilados*) and Angolans from other parts of the country. In October 1961, in the first of several such incidents, UPA troops captured and killed 21 MPLA guerrillas, who were travelling south to reinforce

MPLA units in the Dembos areas north of Luanda. Holden Roberto later confirmed that he had given orders to intercept and annihilate the columns.[2]

The subsequent course of the Angolan war was decisively influenced by events in the former Belgian Congo (Congo-Leopoldville, later Zaire). The natural rear base for guerrilla warfare in Angola, where hundreds of thousands of Angolans had fled in 1961, it was also the scene for the first decisive intervention of the U.S. Central Intelligence Agency (CIA) in African politics. The CIA had orchestrated the ouster of the Congo's first elected leader, Patrice Lumumba, after labelling him a dangerous leftist. U.S. protegé Mobutu, who collaborated in Lumumba's murder in January 1961, played a leading and eventually dominating role in the country's politics. It was not a congenial environment for developing unity among Angolans against U.S. ally Portugal.

Roberto's UPA, with its roots in the Congo exile community, had the advantage, and theoretically could have taken the initiative towards unity. But Roberto had little inclination towards power-sharing, and little understanding of Angola beyond the Kikongo-speaking area of the north. Angolans from other parts of the country in the UPA leadership found themselves sidelined, and unity efforts with other groups repeatedly capsized on Roberto's intransigence.

The MPLA, by contrast, sought consciously to build a national movement, campaigning against tribal and racial division. It too was rooted primarily in one sector of Angolan society—the capital and its Kimbundu-speaking hinterland. But the political perspective of its leadership—radical and in some cases Marxist—dictated an effort to overcome such divisions. In 1962 and 1963, despite functioning in the hostile context of Congo-Leopoldville, the MPLA was winning support among refugees on the basis of its relief and medical services. But it was blocked from resupplying its guerrillas inside Angola. And despite the new leadership of Agostinho Neto (elected MPLA president after escaping from Portugal in 1962), it was diplomatically eclipsed by Roberto, who formed a new front (FNLA) and a government-in-exile with the aid of the Congo government. When they were finally expelled from the Congo (Leopoldville) at the end of 1963, MPLA exiles were divided and discouraged, the movement's fortunes at low ebb.

In addition to his patronage from U.S.-backed Congo leaders Mobutu and Adoula, Roberto managed to join his Congolese friends on the CIA payroll. His military and political force in exile was substantial. But UPA's guerrilla war inside Angola was stagnant, and Roberto apparently had no strategies for changing the situation. The U.S. subsidy he received annoyed the Portuguese, but it was not intended to allow him to challenge them. It was sufficient, however, to strengthen him against the rival MPLA. The U.S. regarded Neto, with his Marxist leanings and international left-wing support, as too much of a threat, even though he was the son of a Methodist pastor and had sought support from the U.S. as well as other countries.

Jonas Savimbi, born in 1934 at Munhango on the Benguela railroad in eastern Angola, was a student in Switzerland when war first broke out in 1961. Affiliating with Holden Roberto, he became secretary-general of UPA and foreign minister for its government-in-exile after 1962. Being from the Ovimbundu, Angola's largest ethnic group, located in the central highlands, Savimbi was seen as giving a more representative character to the UPA leadership. Spending part of his time in Switzerland and part in Leopoldville, Savimbi maneuvered for influence only to be repeatedly frustrated by Roberto.

In July, 1964, at the Organization of African Unity (OAU) summit in Cairo, Savimbi resigned from UPA, denouncing Roberto for "tribal favoritism" and subservience to "American imperialism." Returning to Switzerland, Savimbi completed his *license* (roughly equivalent to a U.S. master's degree) in political science. Although he visited the MPLA in Brazzaville, he declined to join unless offered a top position. Instead, with fellow exiles in Europe and contacts in newly independent Zambia, he laid plans to form a third movement—the National Union for the Total Independence of Angola (UNITA).

The MPLA, meanwhile, used its base in Congo-Brazzaville to build up a guerrilla front in the enclave of Cabinda. It won new backing from the OAU, which had for a time granted exclusive recognition to Roberto's government-in-exile. In 1966 and 1967, clandestinely traversing Zaire, the MPLA succeeded in sending supplies to its guerrillas north of Luanda, despite the arrest and execution of some of its militants by the FNLA. After Zambian independence in October 1964, the MPLA aimed at establishing a third guerrilla front in eastern Angola—precisely the area in which Savimbi was launching his own organization. It would not be long before conflict between the two turned to violence.

John Marcum's influential study of Angolan nationalism has popularized the conception of three ethnic (tribal) strands, each linked to its own movement: the FNLA representing the Kongo, MPLA the Mbundu and UNITA the Ovimbundu. Like all stereotypes, this one has its elements of truth. But Marcum's own details reveal a picture that is much more complex and ambiguous than the summary commonly extracted from them. Uniting people of different languages and backgrounds to build a common vision of a free Angola was indeed a complex and unresolved issue. But the competition was within movements as well as between them, and it was as much one of ideas, personal commitments, and organizational capabilities as one of ethnic loyalties.[3]

How was one to solve the complex problems of building a guerrilla war against long material odds, and sustain commitment to the nascent nation amidst personal problems and internal conflicts of all sorts? How to tie together the different fronts of international diplomacy, of the exiles dispersed in different countries, and the guerrilla struggle in different regions of Angola? Such practical questions were central to sustaining the anticolonial war.

One crucial testing ground was sparsely populated eastern Angola. The local people in these war zones were neither Kongo, nor Mbundu, nor Ovimbundu, but they were eager to fight against Portuguese colonialism and ready to follow fellow Angolans who promised to lead them. Ethnic identity might be one factor in deciding whom to trust, but actions were even more decisive. Sorting out fact from fiction, however, was not easy even on the spot, and the scattered reports of visitors tell different stories. Still, the main outlines of the story are clear, setting a plausible context for the documents of Operation Timber.

The War in the East

"Terras do fim do mundo—the ends of the earth," the Portuguese called these remote districts (now provinces) of Moxico and Cuando Cubango. Moxico alone, with a population of less than 300,000 in 1960, was over twice the size of Portugal. Moxico's capital, Luso, in the late sixties a town of little more than 5,000 inhabitants, was the headquarters for Portugal's counterinsurgency war in the east. In the grasslands and river valleys were the units of guerrillas and the people who had joined them, avoiding Portuguese resettlement campaigns. Some owed allegiance to Jonas Savimbi's UNITA; a larger number to the MPLA. Both organizations had arrived in the province shortly after the independence of neighboring Zambia, in October 1964.

UNITA had been conceived as an organization in Switzerland in late 1964, according to Savimbi.[4] In 1965 and 1966 he and eleven others trained in guerrilla warfare in China, while UNITA contacts in Zambia prepared the ground in eastern Angola. Savimbi himself crossed into Angola in October 1966, six months after the founding conference of UNITA at Muangai, some 140 miles inside Angola. The first attacks, in December 1966, pitted hastily mobilized recruits against Portuguese troops in posts such as Teixeira de Sousa, on the Zaire border. UNITA casualties were high, and thereafter the group rarely ventured such a large-scale attack. With poorly armed and trained guerrillas, it was clear that such tactics were suicidal.

The possibility of more systematic supplies through Zambia was soon blocked after UNITA sabotaged the vulnerable Benguela Railway tracks. The line was vital for the export of Zambian copper and import of supplies for the mines. Savimbi, who had travelled to Egypt and China in search of arms in early 1967, found himself expelled from Zambia on his return in mid-year. After a year of exile in Egypt and Europe, Savimbi slipped back into Angola in July 1968. By that time UNITA had apparently established a base area in the forested headwaters of the Lungu Bungo River, located south of the Benguela Railway west of Luso. The next stop on the railway, just across the district border with Bié, was Munhango, Savimbi's birthplace.

Over the following years, UNITA communiques cited attacks on Portuguese troops moving along the dirt roads of Moxico and Cuando Cubango, with occasional references to locations across the district borders with Bié, Malanje, and Lunda. An occasional journalist—Steve Valentine of the *Times of Zambia* in 1969, Austrian Fritz Sitte in 1971, Leon Dash of the *Washington Post* and several others in 1973— trekked into the UNITA areas. All the visitors appear to have followed roughly the same route—along the Luanguinga river and then to the Lungué-Bungo south of Luso.

It is clear from their testimony that UNITA did control some populated territory. In the vast open spaces of eastern Angola, moreover, UNITA could escort a visitor for days without meeting any Portuguese troops, MPLA guerrillas, or anyone at all except UNITA supporters. But the MPLA, and the Portuguese army as well, could give equally convincing tours. Such testimony alone gave little evidence of overall effectiveness or control.

In fact, according to a variety of sources, UNITA's military activities against the Portuguese were minimal, especially compared to those of the rival MPLA. Secret Portuguese military documents, reporting guerrilla attacks in all of Angola in 1970, attribute 59% to the MPLA, 37% to the FNLA, and only 4% to UNITA.[5] Marcum concluded that after 1970 at least, "UNITA relied largely on a little-combat, low-profile strategy."[6]

The MPLA, in contrast, developed a more systematic and sustained guerrilla campaign against the Portuguese, although it was weakened significantly by Portuguese counterinsurgency efforts and internal divisions after 1972. From 1964 the MPLA began political organizing in eastern Angola, systematically mobilizing support in the rural communities. They also arranged training for recruits in Zambia, Tanzania, Algeria, and Eastern Europe, as well as transferring veterans from the Cabinda front. MPLA organizers tackled the complex logistics of supply over more than two thousand miles of road from Dar es Salaam, Tanzania, the final portion of it through remote western Zambia. The flow of arms, ammunition, medicines and school supplies was little more than a trickle, but it meant that guerrillas and political organizers could offer more than promises to the people they mobilized.

South African journalist Al Venter, visiting eastern Angola with the Portuguese military in 1969, noted that the MPLA was "able to maintain a steady pressure on the Portuguese civil and military authorities."[7] The guerrillas concentrated on road ambushes, he was told. With the exception of a reference to occasional sabotage of the Benguela Railway "between Munhango and Luso . . . [by] what was left of Savimbi's forces in the area," the Portuguese officers briefing Venter made little mention of UNITA.[8]

Visitors to MPLA's eastern front during these years portray a developing guerrilla campaign covering much of Moxico and Cuando Cubango provinces, but also the devastating effects of Portuguese counterinsurgency efforts. Anthropologist Don Barnett and filmmaker Roy Harvey, after attending MPLA's eastern regional conference in August 1968, barely escaped a Portuguese raid which killed Dr. Américo Boavida, head of MPLA's medical program.[9] Historian Basil Davidson, visiting the same area in mid-1970, noted that the guerrillas had serious shortages of weapons, and cited the use of herbicides in the Portuguese campaigns against the guerrilla zones.[10] Henk Odink, who spent six months in MPLA zones in northeastern Moxico in 1972, also noted the use of napalm.[11]

The cornerstones of the counterinsurgency effort were helicopter raids, sometimes with South African support, and a massive force resettlement program, regrouping African peasants into strategic villages. According to the Moxico district governor in 1969, as many as 80 percent of the 140,000 Africans "under guerrilla control" had been recovered.[12] Although these figures were probably exaggerated, such measures imposed a degree of effective repression. They were accompanied by military and secret police recruitment of informers and African paramilitary forces and, as Operation Timber shows, by the use of UNITA against the MPLA.

Under these conditions, the MPLA proved unable to consolidate the east strongly enough to mount more than isolated attacks further west, in the more populous provinces of Bié or Malanje. From 1972, conflict arose between a splinter group led by Daniel Chipenda and cadres loyal to President Agostinho Neto.[13] Because of this, the guerrilla war was much reduced in intensity during the last two years of colonial rule.

Still, Portugal was unable to end the insurgency. Along with the escalating conflicts in Guinea-Bissau and Mozambiqie, it finally provoked the Portuguese army itself to abandon the colonial project. Leading Portuguese novelist António Lobo Antunes, who served on the eastern front in 1971 and 1972, recalled the army's frustration in his novel *Os Cus de Judas*. He paints a picture of the troops sitting in isolated posts or anxiously anticipating ambushes along remote dirt tracks. Meanwhile the Africans imprisoned in the resettlement camps, "spied on by PIDE [International Police for the Defense of the State, the Portuguese secret police], tyranized by the guards, [fled] to the bush where the MPLA, an invisible enemy, was hiding, forcing us into an hallucinatory war of ghosts."[14]

And what of UNITA while the MPLA and the Portuguese were fighting it out? It seems that as early as 1967-1968 UNITA clashes with the MPLA were at least as common as its confrontations with Portuguese troops. None of the published sources gives much detail on these clashes, but it is clear that each movement regarded the east as its rightful zone of operations. Without some kind of agreement, conflict was inevitable.

The MPLA was not open to a rival independent organization headed by Savimbi, who had refused their offer to join in 1964. And Savimbi's hostility to the MPLA was deep-rooted.

Already in 1961, according to an American diplomat cited by Gerald Bender, "Savimbi showed much more hostility toward other rebel groups in Angola than he did against the Portuguese."[15] Savimbi had introduced himself at the U.S. Embassy in Bern as the "future president of Angola," and denounced the MPLA, accusing its leaders of being mulattos disliked by most Angolans. As the Operation Timber documents show, that animosity would lead him into explicit alliance with the Portuguese military.

This outcome stands in glaring contrast to the ultrarevolutionary rhetoric Savimbi and his supporters favored in the same period. In part compensating for his own failure to establish secure outside support, but also repeating a theme he had stressed for some years, Savimbi denounced other Angolan leaders for relying on outside aid and accused them of failing to base the struggle within the country. His claim to be building a movement exclusively on internal support from the peasants and capture of arms from the enemy was attractive to idealistic outsiders. It pleased those who were wary of MPLA ties with the Soviet Union, whether their views stemmed from Western anticommunism or a sympathy for the Chinese side in the Sino-Soviet dispute. It was less romantic to admit that sustained guerrilla warfare depended both on the mobilization of local support and on assuring outside supplies.

Savimbi also won support in some overseas circles by denouncing what he claimed was white and mestiço domination in the MPLA leadership, often lumping urban Kimbundu-speaking blacks into the same category. Describing them as overly influenced by Portuguese culture and not close enough to the common people of Angola, he presented himself as the genuine "black power" peasant leader. Most such supporters broke ranks with him after 1975, when he openly allied himself with South Africa. But few were aware that this opportunistic alliance with apartheid had been prefigured by an earlier deal with Portugal.

Operation Timber: A Summary of the Evidence

In its July 8, 1974 issue, the Paris-based *AfriqueAsie* published translations of four documents (documents 72/6 through 72/9 below), three from Jonas Savimbi to the Portuguese military authorities in eastern Angola, one a reply from Lt. Col. Ramires de Oliveira, chief of staff of the Eastern Military Zone. Dating from September to November 1972, these documents showed, according to *AfriqueAsie*, that Savimbi "has been, at least since 1972, an agent of the Portuguese."

The exposé came shortly after UNITA had signed a cease-fire agreement with Portugal, only two months after the April 25 coup in Lisbon had brought down the regime of Marcello Caetano. At the time neither the MPLA nor the FNLA had yet signed similar cease-fire agreements, nor would they do so until General António Spínola was ousted from power on September 30, 1974. Spínola, who served as Portugal's president after the coup in an uneasy coalition with the officers of the Armed Forces Movement, was dedicated to achieving a pro-Portuguese political settlement in Angola. He rejected the option of total independence for the colony.

Savimbi denounced *AfriqueAsie*, a long-time supporter of the MPLA, for publishing "forgeries."[16] While the accusations against UNITA were widely believed among those sympathetic to the MPLA in Angola, Portugal, and other European countries, neither the Portuguese originals nor English translations of the documents were published at the time.[17] Military and secret police files had been gutted at the time of the coup, and it was not possible to verify the provenance of the documents independently. Most scholars opted then and subsequently for a cautious verdict of "insufficient evidence" on the collaboration the documents revealed.[18]

More than five years later, in November 1979, editor Augusto de Carvalho of the influential *Expresso*, a mainstream Portuguese weekly, published a series of three articles containing the text of other documents—letters, minutes, memoranda—tracing what he identified as "Operation Timber" back to 1971. *Expresso* also related the story of a soldier who had served on the eastern front, whose suspicions were aroused when his commander advised him not to follow up on intelligence providing an opportunity to capture Savimbi. In reply to critics charging a political campaign against Savimbi, the *Expresso* editor asserted "the fact that Savimbi collaborated with the Portuguese colonial authorities ... can no longer be honestly doubted." The paper had "authentic proof," he said, and aimed at giving readers "all the facts."[19] The *Expresso* articles, however, were apparently not picked up at the time in English-language media, nor have I been able to discover any subsequent reference to them by English-speaking scholars.[20]

Finally, in 1985, a book-length account of the affair appeared in Angola, with quotes from a series of documents dating from 1971 through June 1974. The book was illustrated with photographic reproductions of a significant number of the documents. The book had originally been prepared several years earlier as a series of newspaper articles for *Jornal de Angola*, the Angolan daily paper. But publication was delayed, and it was eventually decided to publish them as a book.[21]

The translations published below thus come from a variety of sources (the source is indicated at the beginning of each document). Nevertheless, the cumulative evidence for their authenticity is substantial. The full collection shows a complex and nuanced picture, which repeatedly checks out with other information. And, while neither the participants nor those who leaked the documents are yet willing to speak openly and in detail about the period, a variety of testimonies—from sources with different political perspectives—confirm at least the general outline of Operation Timber. The published sources include the following:

● Pompílio da Cruz, a right-wing Portuguese settler in Angola and active participant in political maneuvering after the April 1974 coup, accuses a leader of the Armed Forces Movement in Angola, General Franco Pinheiro, of leaking the documents. "It was Dr. Franco," he says, "who, disloyally, with the perfidy of a venemous animal, used his official post to provide photocopies of documents exchanged between the Portuguese authorities and Dr. Jonas Savimbi, which the MPLA used as gross destructive posters against the UNITA leader, publishing them in the international press."[22]

• Franz Sitte, a pro-Savimbi Austrian journalist and author of no less than three books detailing his travels with UNITA, published a German translation of the *AfriqueAsie* documents in 1981. He introduced them by noting that the content of the letters could lead to a variety of conclusions. But "the authenticity of the 'Savimbi-letters'," he added, "is doubted by no side."[23] Sitte commented that Savimbi "during the colonial period already had the quite correct premonition of how things would develop after the departure of the Portuguese from Angola and what role the MPLA would play ... Already in 1971 Savimbi told me a very meaningful proverb: If a non-swimmer falls into a flood, he grabs any stick of wood that gives him a chance to be saved."[24]

• Portugal's Prime Minister Marcello Caetano, in a book published not long afer his overthrow in 1974, refers briefly to the military situation in Angola in the early 1970s. He refers to Bettencourt Rodrigues, who was charged with pacifying eastern Angola and "succeeded, including an understanding with UNITA."[25]

• General Costa Gomes, commander-in-chief in Angola from April 1970 through August 1972, and president of Portugal from September 1974 through July 1976, told a journalist in 1979 that UNITA "was practically neutralized, having signed an agreement, in the second half of 1971, leading to suspension of military operations." He added, as the documents confirm, that "later, in the last quarter of 1973, the agreement was violated by us [the Portuguese army], giving rise to increased military activity in the East."[26]

[The period of the documents released by *AfriqueAsie* in 1974, it is interesting to note, is confined to late 1972, including neither the time that Costa Gomes was in Angola nor the episode of UNITA/Portuguese confrontation in late 1973. The full set of documents, however, includes both periods.]

Several Portuguese officers, interviewed by David Martin

and Phyllis Johnson in April and June 1984, confirmed the operation in somewhat greater detail.[27] General Costa Gomes told them that the contact through local woodcutters with UNITA led to a gentlemen's agreement in 1971. It would have been easy to eliminate UNITA's several hundred guerrillas, he said, but from a military point of view it was better to use them against the MPLA. The direct contact with UNITA, he said, was through General Bettencourt Rodrigues and Ramires de Oliveira. Military intelligence chief Passos Ramos was also actively involved. After 1971 there were some small accidental confrontations between UNITA and Portuguese groups, but no important ones until early 1974. He understood that some Portuguese officers started the fighting.

During the term of the agreement, Costa Gomes explained, it was understood that Portuguese and UNITA forces would not fight against each other. UNITA captured food and armaments from the MPLA, while the Portuguese gave them ammunition (not guns), as well as medical and school equipment. The area reserved for UNITA was the Lungué-Bungo river area, between Luso and Bié.

General Bettencourt Rodrigues, although he agreed to an interview, was far more evasive. He conceded that one could assume the documents were genuine, but said it was too soon to discuss such classified material. He was in command of all the forces in the east, and coordinated with PIDE, although it was more or less independent, having its own African fighting corps, the *Flechas*. In response to more questions about the correspondence, he stressed that Savimbi's contacts were with the military, not PIDE. He added that in a subversive war one couldn't necessarily trust written documents.

Two high-level officers who also served in Angola, but who refused to be quoted by name, confirmed the general timetable of an agreement in 1971, briefly interrupted in late 1973 or early in 1974. One of them said that Brigadier Hipólito, who replaced Bettencourt Rodrigues in mid-1973, saw the situation differently, and that tensions with UNITA led to conflict. Referring to attacks around the time of New Year, 1974, one of them contradicted Costa Gomes' version, saying that

UNITA had broken the agreement first, not the Portuguese. After April 25 new talks with UNITA resulted in the June 14 cease-fire agreement, said one of the officers, who had served in the Portuguese delegation to the talks. The general outline of Operation Timber is thus confirmed by a variety of sources. With that established, the detail in the documentation, much of it extraneous to what a hypothetical forger might include to discredit Savimbi, provides additional credibility.

The contacts revealed in the documents begin with correspondence between UNITA sector chief Edmundo Rocha and two Portuguese timber merchants, Zeca Oliveira and António Duarte (Documents 71/1 through 71/6). [Previous contacts between PIDE and UNITA are referred to in Documents 72/2, 72/3 and an anonymous letter to *Expresso*, reproduced in Appendix IIA. There have also been charges that Savimbi was even encouraged to form UNITA by the director of PIDE in Angola, Anibal de São José Lopes. But no documentary evidence has emerged for that early period.] These contacts by themselves show no more than the kind of *modus vivendi* any guerrilla movement would seek with those operating in its area. And Savimbi acknowledges such contacts.[28] He says that UNITA, through arrangements with timber merchants, sought "to exploit the weak points of the colonial structure, in the areas of Cangumbe, Luso and Léau." He also acknowledges that these loggers maintained contacts with PIDE.

The November 10 memorandum of the DGS (secret police, formerly called PIDE), raises the prospect of a more intimate relationship than local contacts with timber merchants. In noting that UNITA's "strategy is directly solely for survival," the DGS evaluation anticipated that Savimbi might be ready for a deal. The governor-general's approval (Document 71/8) set the scene for formal establishment of "Working Group Timber," chaired by General Bettencourt Rodrigues, commander of the Eastern Military Zone.

The minutes of the working group (Document 71/10) and the first letters signed by Savimbi himself (Documents 72/1, 72/2), as well as subsequent documents from early 1972, show some uncertainty and hesitation on both sides as the terms of the agreement are worked out. Savimbi's undated letter—written, by the context, in late January or early February—is particularly long-winded and defensive. But it concludes with specific proposals for closer collaboration: a "status-quo" arrangement in UNITA base areas south of the Luso-Munhango road, and cooperation against enemy targets in other zones, with UNITA providing "guides."

By the time of the September-November documents (Documents 72/6 to 72/9, the ones released by *AfriqueAsie*), cooperation was apparently well established, with Savimbi providing specific reports along with his more discursive remarks. Lt. Col. Ramires de Oliveira, in his November 4 reply to Savimbi (Document 72/8), explained that the necessity for secrecy impeded wider freedom of movement for UNITA. "Each time the corridor [to Zambia] is used, it is necessary to inform the Command, so that we can remove Our Troops from the area under some pretext."[29]

These late 1972 documents, while they are written in the same style and entirely consistent with the others, are the most explicitly damning of the whole collection. This seems to confirm rather than to challenge the authenticity, since it is more consistent with someone *choosing* them to leak than with preparation of forgeries. If the documents were forged, it would make little sense to release—years later—additional ones with less dramatic revelations.

The two documents from 1973 come from the period of transition between Gen. Bettencourt Rodrigues and his successor Barroso Hipólito. Appropriately, they are a bureaucratic reformulation of the bases of the operation, in the form of a letter to Savimbi and a directive to the military authorities involved.

But the guidelines apparently did not prevent the development of misunderstandings. Sabino Sandele's handwritten letter of January 8, 1974, to timber merchant Oliveira (Document 74/1) complains of Portuguese attacks against UNITA base areas in violation of the agreement. UNITA communiqués at the time referred to New Year's Day attacks on barracks at Luando and Alto Cuito, as well as a January 20th raid on Muangai.[30] In his 1979 book, Savimbi says that

UNITA launched a new offensive against the Portuguese in September 1973, but this is neither confirmed nor contradicted by the documents available.[31] And it is unclear whether this was a response to attacks by the Portuguese troops under their new commander.

What is confirmed, in a Portuguese military report of February 21, 1974 (Document 74/7), is that Operation Timber was officially cancelled by the authorities on January 7, and that new talks were initiated, again through timber merchant Zeca Oliveira. Father Araujo de Oliveira, a Portuguese priest in Luso who had also maintained contact with UNITA, was involved as well. It was these contacts, begun before the April coup, that culminated in the June 14 cease-fire.[32] The three pages of the minutes of the cease-fire meeting that are available (Document 74/10), contain several references to Operation Timber, used as a basis for defining the areas and terms of the cease-fire.

Thus the Operation Timber connection gave Savimbi a headstart on the political maneuvering following the Portuguese coup. For the next four months UNITA, unlike the FNLA or MPLA, would be permitted to operate openly in Angola.

Savimbi, South Africa, and the Reagan Doctrine

The course of events after mid-1974, up to the current role of UNITA in South Africa's war against the southern African region, is beyond the limited scope of this short book. But a brief summary is in order, for it is in the light of subsequent developments that Operation Timber becomes more than an interesting historical footnote. In the thirteen years since that June cease-fire Savimbi has become South Africa's most important military client, as well as the darling of the U.S. far right, with additional backers in both the Democratic and Republican parties.

Act I of this new drama began with the April 1974 coup in Lisbon. It was brought to a close by the defeat in March 1976, with the aid of Cuban troops, of the CIA-backed South African invasion of Angola. Act II is running still, a campaign against the MPLA-led People's Republic of Angola involving periodic invasions by South African troops as well as UNITA guerrilla actions. The U.S., which enjoys the dubious distinctions of having backed Portuguese colonialism and encouraged the South Africans to invade in 1975, has since 1986 openly provided an annual subsidy of over $15 million for Savimbi's contra crusade.

In the second half of 1974, UNITA initially sought backing from conservative white settlers in Angola, simultaneously taking advantage of its early cease-fire to mobilize the Ovimbundu on the basis of ethnic loyalty. At the same time the CIA stepped up subsidies to Holden Roberto's FNLA, its long-time client in Zaire, which also gained some aid from China. The MPLA, recovering from internal dissension to regroup around Agostinho Neto (Daniel Chipenda was formally expelled in December), mobilized its followers most successfully in Luanda. The MPLA also won supporters among students, intellectuals, and urban workers of all ethnic groups around the country. And it succeeded in persuading the Soviet Union to resume arms shipments that had been suspended.

Portuguese President Spínola and Zaire President Mobutu met secretly in September of that year, reportedly plotting an Angolan coalition excluding Neto's MPLA. Spínola lost his post later that month, when a far-right plot to oust his leftist opponents backfired, and the scheme was temporarily checked. But Roberto's FNLA, with the aid of Zaire and the CIA, went ahead to strengthen its troops in Angola.

By late 1974, a compromise had emerged among the three nationalist groups recognized by the Organization of African Unity. Meeting with Portuguese representatives in Alvor, Portugal, in January 1975, the MPLA, the FNLA, and UNITA agreed to schedule independence for November 11. In the interim a quadripartite transitional government would administer the country and hold elections for a constituent assembly.

Given the conflicting objectives and mistrust among the

parties, and the fact that no outside power held the ring, it seems unlikely that the Alvor agreement could have been implemented under the best of circumstances. If it had, one can speculate, the contest would still have been over the basis of political competition itself, as well as over who would occupy the seats of power. A campaign based primarily on ethnic and regional appeal would have favored UNITA. If everyone voted according to the ethnic stereotypes, UNITA would have had an estimated 40% to 45%, MPLA 35% to 40%, and FNLA the remainder. If a functioning interim administration had permitted the MPLA to mobilize grass-roots activism and carry out development programs, however, it is likely that it would have substantially expanded its support in the presumed territory of the other groups. But neither scenario was to take place.

The year 1975 instead saw a step-by-step escalation of violence in which internal conflict merged with external intervention, in a sequence that is still the subject of bitter dispute. John Stockwell, who headed the CIA task force in the Angolan intervention from the end of July 1975, later noted that each major escalation was initiated by the United States and its allies.[33]

Before August 1975, external involvement was limited. The major conflict was the bitter fighting between FNLA and MPLA in and around the capital Luanda, particularly in March, April, and July. The FNLA, encouraged by a grant of $300,000 from the CIA shortly after the Alvor Accord, initiated the fighting, relying on its superior conventional military force and its open access to the Zaire border. The MPLA concentrated on mobilizing and arming its supporters, scrambling to get arms in by sea or air despite official Portuguese prohibitions. There is little doubt that the major external involvement in this period came from Zaire, although in mid-year the MPLA received several hundred Cuban military advisers to help train its new recruits.

UNITA, with no significant external support, did not join in the fighting during this period. Savimbi's supporters in Portugal had been weakened by Spínola's ouster. In Angola Portuguese authority was declining, and an increasing number of white settlers fled the country. Some in UNITA argued for reaching an alliance with the MPLA against the FNLA. But Savimbi rejected this option, instead joining Roberto on the CIA payroll and appealing to South Africa for support. Savimbi declared himself opposed to guerrilla warfare against white-minority regimes,[34] and South African advisers began training his forces during that period. In July the U.S. National Security Council allocated an additional $14 million for FNLA and UNITA, and the CIA sought successfully to draw South Africa into a more active role in the conflict. In August, South African troops occupied the area of Calueque, in Cunene province.

In October 1975 thousands of South African troops, along with mercenaries and UNITA and FNLA forces, launched a massive assault aimed at Luanda. The South African invasion from the south, coordinated in advance with the U.S.,[35] complemented the FNLA and Zaire offensive from the north. It was this combined threat that led the MPLA to call for large scale assistance from Cuba. Cuba airlifted thousands of troops to Angola to help repel the attack. As the covert South African role was revealed, African opinion rallied to the side of the MPLA, and U.S. public opinion pushed Congress to curb CIA involvement in Angola with passage of the Clark amendment. In March 1976, South Africa, feeling betrayed by Washington, withdrew the main body of its troops from Angola.

The U.S. intervention in this period nevertheless had a lasting effect. Although most foreign policy professionals and U.S. businessmen involved in Angola argued that the U.S. could deal with the MPLA leadership, Kissinger had gone ahead with the intervention, firing two assistant secretaries of state for Africa who disagreed.[36] His action—and the Soviet response—made the conflict a symbol of the global contest with the Soviet Union. For many in Washington, the defeat became a affront to U.S. pride, particularly aggravating because of the role of Cuban troops. In subsequent months almost every country in the world recognized the MPLA-led People's Republic of Angola. But the U.S. joined South Africa in refusing to accept its legitimacy.

In the aftermath of Angolan independence, the South West African People's Organization (SWAPO) stepped up its guerrilla war for the independence of South African-occupied Namibia. South Africa showed no signs of withdrawing from the territory, which the World Court had ruled illegally occupied in 1971, after decades of South African flouting of UN resolutions. South Africa expanded its troop concentrations in northern Namibia, just south of the Angolan border. Since then South African attacks on Angola have most commonly been justified as hot pursuit or preventive action against SWAPO infiltration.

Before 1980 such actions were relatively small-scale, in comparison to the 1975 invasion or the most recent conflict. Of South Africa's Angolan clients, the FNLA largely disintegrated. Holden Roberto lived on in exile in Zaire and then in France. His right-hand aide, Johnny Eduardo, eventually was reconciled to the new government and returned to Angola. Daniel Chipenda, whose forces had joined the FNLA after he was expelled from the MPLA, went to live in Portugal (He returned to Angola at the end of 1987). But South Africa set up a special unit, the 32 [Three-Two] Batallion, to recruit Angolans into its army. The unit, mainly composed of ex-FNLA soldiers, with a sprinkling of white mercenaries, was subsequently used both in northern Namibia and in southern Angola.

Savimbi and many of his followers fled into the bush; some went to South African training camps in Namibia. While 32 Batallion functioned for the most part close to the border, UNITA operations ranged more widely, into Moxico, Bié, and Huambo provinces. In the areas of combat, some local people first joined UNITA voluntarily. Over the next few years, however, large numbers returned to government zones of control. Many UNITA guerrillas accepted government offers of amnesty. UNITA increasingly resorted to force to recruit its followers, and targeted civilians in government areas. South Africa supplied training, arms, and logistics.

In early 1981 two deserters from 32 Batallion, a British mercenary and an Angolan, described how their unit swept through villages in southern Angola, killing women and children. Working closely with UNITA, they sometimes carried out operations later claimed by UNITA. But in general there was a division of labor. "The 32 Batallion and UNITA had separate spheres of operation," said one of the deserters, "but the same boss—South Africa."[37]

By 1980, the Angolan government had the upper hand, and UNITA guerrilla actions were considerably reduced. But then South Africa greatly escalated its attacks on Angola. The integration of UNITA with the South African military became even closer. Joint operations became more common.

Successive invasions cleared much of Cunene and Cuando Cubango provinces, capturing villages and installing UNITA bases with regular supply links for fuel and ammunition. A stage-set capital was built at Jamba, just north of the Namibian border, and frequent visits arranged for reporters and UNITA supporters overseas. South African troops aided UNITA in capturing Mavinga (1980) and Cangamba (1982). And UNITA acquired a conventional military force, stationed in this protected zone of southeastern Angola. Whenever UNITA proved unable to resist the strengthened Angolan government forces, as in the large-scale battles of 1985 and 1987, South Africa brought in not only the air force but also ground troops and artillery units. On the Angolan government side, Cuban troops remained in rear-guard positions north of the major combat zones.[38]

Beyond this zone of control, UNITA guerrillas and elite South African commandos attacked strategic economic targets and waged a campaign of terror against civilians. In May, 1985, for example, a South African commando was captured in an attempt to blow up Gulf Oil installations in Cabinda. At an international news conference he admitted UNITA was set to take credit for the operation. UNITA adopted the practice of planting land mines in the fields and on paths used by peasants, in an effort to force peasants to flee to UNITA zones and to disrupt the country's food production. On a number of occasions, UNITA guerrillas massacred large numbers of civilians in government-controlled villages.[39]

The group undoubtedly retained some support on ethnic

grounds. But significant numbers of the Angolan army were themselves from the same ethnic groups. A regular flow of deserters from UNITA accepting the government amnesty was accompanied by occasional reports of execution of opponents of Savimbi who considered ending the war.[40] UNITA's targeting of civilians, food production, and health services made little sense if it really had the support of the civilian population. But such tactics fitted perfectly into South Africa's strategy of terrorizing and destabilizing neighboring countries.

It also corresponded to the premise of Reagan conservatives that any tactics were acceptable against a regime which had close ties with Cuba and the Soviet Union. But the U.S. hostility against the Luanda government was broader than these extreme-right circles.

For ten years after the 1975-1976 intervention, U.S. involvement in the war in Angola was legally forbidden by the Clark amendment. U.S. oil companies and other U.S. businesses established good working relations with the government in Luanda. But efforts by some Carter administration officials to shift policy toward diplomatic recognition lost out in Washington. And, although the details are still obscure, it is almost certain that other U.S. officials violated at least the spirit of the Clark amendment, by encouraging other countries to aid Savimbi. Pro-Savimbi journalist Bridgland cites Morocco and Saudi Arabia, as well as Zaire, as particularly important in this regard.[41]

But U.S. encouragement of UNITA escalated dramatically in 1981, when the Reagan administration took office. Although the Africa Bureau in the State Department took a more cautious line, and the Clark amendment was not repealed by Congress until 1985, the Saudis were apparently encouraged to increase their aid.[42] And the U.S. tilt to South Africa with "constructive engagement" encouraged stepped-up South African involvement. Finally, in 1986 and 1987 the U.S. supplied at least $30 million in covert military aid to Savimbi, including Stinger missiles.

Like one of his patrons, Ronald Reagan, with whom Savimbi shares an enormous poster in his capital of Jamba,

Savimbi's public relations skills seem to protect him from serious scrutiny, at least in Washington. Many who profess to abhor apartheid see no contradiction in aiding South Africa's contra warrior in Angola, even when he chides South African Blacks for their ungrateful rejection of Botha's reform.[43] History will eventually demystify him, but the process must begin now. Along with the ongoing collaboration with South Africa, "Operation Timber" is a chapter that anyone trying to understand Angola today must confront.

Notes

1. Gerald J. Bender, *Angola under the Portuguese* (Berkeley: University of California Press, 1978), p. 65; Basil Davidson, *In the Eye of the Storm: Angola's People* (Garden City, NY: Doubleday, 1973), p. 94.

2. John Marcum, *The Angolan Revolution, Vol. I* (Cambridge: MIT Press, 1969), p. 214.

3. These issues are explored in fictional form by Angolan novelist Pepetela, who served as an MPLA guerrilla commander, in his novel *Maiombe*, set in Cabinda. Although the novel raised delicate issues, President Agostinho Neto strongly encouraged its publication. See the English translation *Mayombe*, by Artur Pestana (Pepetela), published by Zimbabwe Publishing House and by Heinemann.

4. Jonas Malheiro Savimbi, *Angola: A Resistência em Busca de Uma Nova Nação* (Lisboa: Agência Portuguesa de Revistas, 1979), p. 19.

5. *De Groene Amsterdammer*, July 11, 1973, in *Facts & Reports*, August 18, 1973.

6. John Marcum, *The Angolan Revolution, v. II* (Cambridge: MIT Press, 1978), p. 217.

7. Al J. Venter, *The Terror Fighters*, (Cape Town: Purnell, 1969), p. 120.

8. *Ibid.*, p. 131.

9. Don Barnett and Roy Harvey, *The Revolution in Angola: MPLA, Life Histories and Documents* (Indianapolis: Bobbs-Merrill, 1972).

10. Davidson, p. 278.

11. Henk Odink, *De Overwinning is Zeker: Reisverlag an een Verblijf bij de Volksbeweging voor de Bevrijding van Angola*, (Amsterdam: Uitgave Medisch Komitee Angola, 1974), p. 30.

12. Gerald J. Bender, "The Limits of Counterinsurgency: An African Case," in *Comparative Politics* (4:3, April 1972), p. 341.

13. Daniel Chipenda, the most prominent MPLA leader of Ovimbundu origin, was expelled from the MPLA at the end of 1974, taking some of his followers the next year into the ranks of the FNLA, and joining in the conflict against the MPLA in 1975-1976. Later he lived in exile in Portugal, but has recently been reconciled with the MPLA government in Luanda.

14. António Lobo Antunes, *Os Cus de Judas* (Lisboa: Publicações Dom Quixote, 1969), p. 48. The title "Judas' Ass" is less explicitly rendered in the English translation *South of Nowhere*, published by Random House in 1983.

15. Gerald J. Bender, "Angola: Left, Right & Wrong," in *Foreign Policy* (43: Summer, 1981), p. 59.

16. Agence France Presse, September 6, 1974, in *Facts and Reports*, September 14, 1974. Also Fred Bridgland, *Jonas Savimbi: A Key to Africa* (New York: Paragon House, 1987), p. 107.

17. Abridged translations of the four, plus two others, were published by Pravda correspondent Oleg Ignatyev in *Secret Weapon in Africa* (published in English in 1977 by Progress Publishers in Moscow). The four in *AfriqueAsie* were translated and published in 1979 in *Dirty Work 2: The CIA in Africa*, edited by Ellen Ray, William Schaap, Karl van Meter and Louis Wolf (Secaucus, NJ: Lyle Stuart).

18. See John Marcum's reference to "what purported to be copies of (1972) letters detailing UNITA-Portuguese collusion" (John Marcum, *The Angolan Revolution, Vol. II*, p. 248). F.W. Heimer, however, one of the best informed foreign scholars on Angola, concluded that "the evidence available at present does not yet appear reliable/conclusive enough to establish the exact nature of the relationship between UNITA and the Portuguese colonial army (and political police), but proves the existence of such a relationship." (F.W. Heimer, *The Decolonization Conflict in Angola, 1974-76*, Geneva: Institut Universitaire de Hautes Etudes Internationales, 1979, p. 31).

19. *Expresso*, November 30, 1979. The other two articles were in the November 17 and November 24 issues.

20. John Marcum's second volume was published in 1978, before the *Expresso* articles, as was Gerald J. Bender's *Angola under the Portuguese* (Berkeley: University of California Press, 1978). Fred Bridgland's Savimbi biography does not cite the articles, nor does a lengthy pro-Savimbi dissertation on *The UNITA Insurgency in Angola* by W. Martin James, III (Catholic University, 1986). James, like Bridgland, appears to have consulted few if any sources at all in the Portuguese language.

21. R. Sotto-Maior, *História de Uma Traição* (Luanda: Alvorada Editora, 1985). Information on publication from interview with author in Luanda, July 1987.

22. Pompílio da Cruz, *Vivos e Mortos* (Lisboa: Intervenção, 1976), pp. 159-160.

23. Franz Sitte, *Flug in der Angola-Hoelle: Der Vergessene Krieg* (Graz: Verlag Styria, 1981), p. 137.
24. *Ibid.*, p. 151.
25. Marcella Caetano, *Depoimento* (Rio de Janeiro: Distribuidora Record), 1974, pp. 180-181.
26. Costa Gomes, *Sobre Portugal: Diálogos com Alexandre Manuel*, (Lisboa: A Regra do Jogo, 1979), p. 32.
27. I was allowed to use the notes of these interviews on the condition of observing the original terms of the interviews: quotes are indirect, not exact words, and two of the interviewees remained anonymous.
28. Savimbi, *op. cit.*, pp. 37-39.
29. This secrecy also implied, it would seem, that the majority of the ordinary soldiers on both sides were not informed of the arrangement, and that as a consequence there were occasional "accidental" clashes.
30. *Times of Zambia*, March 6, 1974.
31. Savimbi, *op. cit.*, pp. 29-30.
32. The date is given in some sources as June 17, but that was the date of the Portuguese announcement, not of the actual signing.
33. John Stockwell, *In Search of Enemies* (New York: W.W. Norton, 1978), pp. 66-67.
34. Johannesburg *Star*, May 3, 1975.
35. Wayne Smith, "A Trap in Angola," in *Foreign Policy*, Spring 1986, p. 72.
36. See Gerald Bender, "Kissinger in Angola: Anatomy of Failure," pp. 63-43 in Rene Lemarchand, ed., *American Foreign in Southern Africa: The Stakes and the Stance, Second Edition* (Washington: University Press of America, 1981); also Nathaniel Davis, "The Angola Decision of 1975: A Personal Memoir," in *Foreign Affairs* 57 (Fall 1978), pp. 109-124.
37. See *Guardian* (London), January 29 and February 2, 1981; *Africa News*, March 23, 1981. The British mercenary wsa named Trevor Edwards, the Angolan Jose Ricardo Belmundo. For additional quotes from an interview with Belmundo, see Appendix 2.
38. The deceptive reporting of the war in Angola is particularly clear in the coverage of the 1987 fighting. Most press reports came from South African or UNITA sources, and one would have gathered from these reports that UNITA alone was gaining a great victory against MPLA troops backed by large numbers of Cubans and Soviets. Only after South African white casualties rose so high that they could no longer deny them did South Africa admit, and the U.S. press report, that South African troops had been involved on a large scale. (*Washington Post*, November 12 and 13, 1987; *New York Times*, November 16, 1987). Ironically, the conservative *Washington Times*, less embarrassed perhaps by the South African connection, reported it in some detail in earlier articles (September 30, October 5, October 6). For more accurate reporting see, for example, the weekly newsletter *Southscan* (London), October 7, November 18, and November 25, 1987.

39. See, for example, references in *Washington Post*, July 29, 1986; March 15, 1987; Cherri Waters, *Angola: A Matter of Justice* (New York: National Council of Churches, 1987), pp. 24-25.
40. *New York Times*, December 27, 1987.
41. Bridgland, *op. cit.*, pp. 256-258, 273-274, 286-291.
42. *New York Times*, June 21, 1987.
43. *New York Times*, June 7, 1987.

Pro-UNITA demonstration in Luanda, 1974.

General Joaquim Luz Cunha

EXMO SENHOR ARMÉNIO NUNO RAMIRES DE OLIVEIRA
TEN: COR. DO CEM
- CHEFE DO ESTADO MAIOR ZMLeste

LUSO

Pedi há dias ao nosso Capitão Clemente para dirigir uma nota a
VExa para agradecer a cedência das munições cal.7,62 e mais para pa-
tentear o nosso agrado ao ver que cada reunião tem nos levado mais
próximos dos objectivos maiores que todos nós queremos atingir.Por
meio desta cumpre-me enviar o duplicado da nota no 3081/2 de 30/9/72
devidamente assinado segundo se estipulava no canto superior direito
da mesma nota.

Já foi efectuada uma acção contra os homens da UPA aos 12/10/72
que nos proporcionou os seguintes resultados:6 armas capturadas todas
PM baretta,5 minas anti-pessoal,3 granadas de morteiro 60mm,250 balas
de diversos calibres e fardamento vário.Uma vez reconhecido o acampa-
mento referenciado nas duas notas que VExa teve a amabilidade de nos
enviar,constactou-se que os homens da UPA tinham-se deslocado.Para não
se perder mais tempo,então o nosso grupo de combate perseguiu os mesmos
tendo os encontrado em SUTA,num riacho chamado "IMONOMONO" que é um
tributário do R CASSAI.Mas como soube-se que eles tem tido muitos contactos com as populações que habitam nas imediações,os nossos grupos de
combate continuam na area e conto instruí-los a ficarem lá até fins do
mês de Novembro para vermos se poderemos obter maiores resultados até
mesmo destruir as suas estructuras.Isto figura na area 1.

No dia 13/10/72 as nossas forças executaram uma operação contra
os homens do MPLA.Um grupo formado de 20 homens sendo apenas 17 armados
tinha-se infiltrado nas nossas areas sem que podessemos dar com eles.Uma
vez praticados os seus desmandos habituais,retiraram-se em direcção ao
Quambo.Foi esta razão que não me deu mais tempo para avisar o COMANDO da
ZML.Assim os nossos homens tiveram de perseguir o IN ate em CASSINGO.Uma
vez encontrados em plena dança"MAKOPO" foram violentamente atacados.A o-
peração forneceu-nos os seguintes resultados:1 PM chinesa,1 PM 44, 1 lan-
ça-foguetes 40mm com duas granadas,15 granadas tipo chinês com cabo de madeira,185 balas de carabina,tendas e fardamento diverso.Os nossos homens
obtiveram a informação de que se encontravam na mesma area mais três acampamentos inimigos nos rios CARILONGUE,LUELA,e finalmente em CHISSIMBA.
Cada um dos acampamentos assinalados não tem mais de 20 guerrilheiros
no máximo.Por isso pede-se a SEXA o General Comandante da ZMA a permis-
são para as nossas forças actuarem na area 2 e 3 a partir do dia 5 de
Novembro de 1972 por um periodo de 1 mês o maximo ou até que se efectua
uma acção para as nossas forças se retirarem imediatamente depois.

Isso marcar o proximo encontro pelo simples facto de que muitos pontos do
seu memorandum ficaram por estudar pelas altas Autoridades Estaduais.Espero
receber alguma informação a esse respeito para que eu possa ir ainda mais
longe na elaboração das minhas ideias.

Aproveito esta oportunidade para enviar a Sua Excelencia o Engenheiro
SANTUS E CASTRO os nossos respeitosos cumprimentos pela sua nomeção para o
alto cargo de Governador-Geral de Angola.

Respeitosamente,
Jonas Malheiro Savimbi,Vic.C.P-J.

Document 72/7

MATCHMAKING: SEPTEMBER–OCTOBER 1971

DOCUMENT 71/1
Kind of Document: Letter
From: Edmundo Rocha, UNITA Sector Chief
To: Zeca Oliveira, timber merchant
Date: September 1, 1971
Source: *Expresso*, November 17, 1979

My Dear Friend Mr. Zeca,
    This is the second time that I am sending you a letter.
    This is not surprising. There are reasons which could be of interest to you since I believe you are one of the loggers of the region.
    I do not have anything to confirm with this letter except to renew the proposals made by one of my colleagues to your overseer. As I do not have any confirmation to date whether you will be interested or not in cooperating with us, I am just conveying to you the following:
    1) It is a tacit fact for any sensible person that there is war in Angola. Even though some may not want to accept the evidence of this fact the truth is that not even the troops are able to eliminate the guerrillas and a good ten years have passed by and not even the Angolan economy in the east has ceased to be seriously affected by this same war. However we are interested in limiting the damage wherever it is possible. In the logging sector, it is possible to make arrangements as long as the parties comply. There have been serious events in this area as well as nearer to Luso[1], only because our contractors were not loyal. And as they were dealing with PIDE[2], their aim was not woodcutting but capturing certain officials of our movement. Now if you are interested in continuing woodcutting within the dictates that our movement can eventually establish for you, you can be assured that there will be nothing to be feared. But beforehand we should tell you the following:

33

2) Not to initiate new routes in the direction of the bush where people who live with us usually go. Should there be agreements and there is need on your part for new cuts then we will have to talk again.
3) To arrange serious overseers who do not compromise you. Since on many occasions quarrels have arisen from the irresponsible behavior of your overseer. Instruct them not to receive any merchandise from the bush outside of the channel that we will establish should it interest you.
4) Without frightening you, I also want to state that it no longer matters how many rural guards protect the vehicles because with time the quantity and quality of our armed forces have increased. If up to now nothing has happened against your trucks, it is because we want to avoid making unnecessary enemies. The air force passed by here to drive away our people. Despite this, and especially because there are limits to the action of an air force, we are going to stop planning hastily.

Having said this I believe that you will know how to defend your own interests and it is not after 10 years of war that you would sacrifice that which is yours by the idle chatter of the authorities who have their bread guaranteed whether there is war or not.

It is all that I have to say today.

Edmundo Rocha

[1] Luso, now called Luena, was the capital of Moxico district (now Moxico province), and the headquarters of the Eastern Military Zone. It is the last major stop on the Benguela Railway, about 160 miles along the railway from the border with Zaire in the east, and about the same distance—as the crow flies—from the Zambian border to the southeast.
[2] PIDE (International Police for the Defense of the State) was the Portuguese secret police. After Marcelo Caetano succeeded the long-lived dictator Salazar in 1968, it was renamed the DGS (General Directorate for Security) in December, 1969. Most people, however, continued to refer to it as PIDE.

DOCUMENT 71/2
Kind of Document: Letter
From: Zeca Oliveira
To: Edmundo Rocha
Date: September 11, 1971
Source: *Expresso*, November 17, 1979

Even though I received your first letter I could not answer

immediately because my partner was not here and I alone cannot make any commitment.

Since my partner is now here and you have written to me again, I am replying. You said in your second letter that there is war in Angola. If this is the case, it is because some people with bad intent want it so, causing confusion and spoiling this land where we always lived in peace. It seems to us from your letter that you are trying to come to an agreement possibly because you feel difficulties and we are willing to talk, but before anything else we want to tell you that we will only talk in serious and constructive terms that take the future into account and not seek a momentary solution.

I am writing to you without the backing or knowledge of our authorities, whether they be civil or military, but I know that if the agreement that you seek aims at an unconditional, honest collaboration and for the future, then they possibly will not think ill of us.

As far as we are concerned this agreement should settle upon the following:

We agree to help you with 2000$00 per month[1] but with the condition that we may cut wood in all the demarcated area that extends to the Lungué Bungo River.

We do not accept your limitations in the logging areas in the area and the concession having been given to us and not to you.

Concerning the people who are in the bush, they can also work perfectly well in logging if duly remunerated; once you are seeking approximation, rancor and old issues should be forgotten, and whites, blacks, and mestiços work together for the common good and the growth and development of Angola.

We will all collaborate in the struggle against UPA[2] and MPLA[3] which are influenced by foreign countries attempting to ruin our Angola, making so many victims among the innocent population.

Angola always belonged to the blacks and whites working together for the common good, and that is how it should always be. I know that our authorities have firmly decided and are striving toward economic and social development which is beginning to be felt everywhere. Let us also work for growth and stop spying on each other in the bush so as to kill each other.

If this is truly your intention then you can count entirely on our collaboration and that of our authorities because I am certain that they are struggling for this ideal of work and growth in peace, overlooking the past, which is to be forgotten, with the promise of finally working in peace and for progress.

If our agreement settles upon the objectives referred to above, you can count on me and my partner. If our ideal is something else and is only destined to resolve a problem of the moment or a particular local situation, then we cannot reach any agreement, therefore, our exchange of correspondence will no longer be necessary.

[1] Two thousand escudos, equivalent to approximately 70 U.S. dollars.
[2] UPA is the acronym for Union of Peoples of Angola, the movement headed by Holden Roberto. UPA was the principal force in the FNLA (National Front for the Liberation of Angola), also formed by Holden Roberto, and in the GRAE (Government of the Republic of Angola in Exile), which Roberto formed to try to gain recognition from African countries.
[3] MPLA stands for Popular Movement for the Liberation of Angola, the movement headed by Agostinho Neto.

DOCUMENT 71/3
Kind of Document: Letter
From: Edmundo Rocha, UNITA Sector Chief
To: Zeca Oliveira, timber merchant
Date: September 14, 1971
Source: Expresso, November 17, 1979

I am not going to contradict your position of no more correspondence. Nevertheless, there are in your letter of the 11th of this month certain relevant points that cannot be clarified without another letter from me. You may not respond but I want to be sure that you received this letter and will give me good advice on how to act should my bosses be interested in the content of this letter.

1) Regarding the extent of your logging operations I am going to make a sketch which I will give to my superiors. In principle, I believe it is within the above limits. But since there are references to the cultivated fields I will have to be precise. The response, for which there is no hurry at all, will only be given to your overseer to avoid unnecessary correspondence.

2) Not only can we provide wax [1] in exchange for merchandise but we also have large puma skins which, in spite of their official sale being prohibited by law, are merchandise that sell well. If so, let us know so that when we begin to send wax we include skins also.

3) We cannot accept that sales are only undertaken with the overseer unless he is serious. We have already had experiences with overseers who diverted the fruit of our sales. This always causes offense. As your overseer has instructions from you to deal with us seriously, we also can guarantee that we will never break the agreement.

4) As proof that the agreement has been accepted, here are 500$00 for certain supplies the list of which is going with the money to the overseer. If on your part the agreement begins this month, I hope that on returning these articles you send me the amount

promised which we will accept as an instrument of contract. With the same money we will shop for you.

5) It is not within my powers to authorize the people who are here in the bush to work in logging. In the meantime, I communicated your proposal to the appropriate person, and we are awaiting a reply.

6) On the political question:

a) We never preached that Angola was only for the Blacks. We know Angola like any Angolan if not better; we know that the Angolan nation is made up of the black majority, mestiços and whites. According to our political outlook, not only those who were born and live here are considered Angolans, as far as white people are concerned, but all those who choose Angola as their motherland. If we were racists as is disseminated throughout Angola with ulterior motives, we would not have released a white woman and a child captured in an ambush in Luangirico against rural guards.[2] We know that after living a month with us, her honor as a woman was respected, and she was taken to Zambia where her wounds were treated by our nurses and sent to Portugal. We know that today she is returning to Luso. Is the Portuguese government capable of capturing a "terrorist" from UNITA carrying arms and giving him back his freedom to live in the bush? It remains to be seen . . . !

b) Regarding our possible cooperation in the struggle against the MPLA or even the UPA, we were always ready for such cooperation since UNITA has never been interested in mistreating the population which is the backbone of the still underdeveloped Angolan economy. If you could tell me how this is possible, I am sure I will be able to convey to my superiors more precise information. As far as our integration is concerned, sooner or later we will become friends. The most important thing is time which shows ways and indicates guidelines. I consider this matter very important and this in particular led me to write to you. Please reply on the matter at your convenience.

Concerning the Angolan economy, I am not convinced with your argument because I know that the Angolan economic situation is different. The superficial aspects of an economy are not sufficient for it to be healthy. What role does the dollar crisis, the drop of the coffee price, the balance of payments always in deficit, transfers, etc., play in the Angolan economy? We will enter this interesting but delicate issue on the next occasion.

Edmundo Rocha

[1] Beeswax, one of the major export products of eastern Angola in the 19th century and still traded, although on a lesser scale, in the 20th century.

2A reference to an incident in 1970. Maria Adelina Neto and her daughter were released in Zambia after a 45-day march through the bush (*The Guardian*, London, December 24, 1970). Luangarico is northwest of Luso.

DOCUMENT 71/4
Kind of Document: Letter
From: Zeca Oliveira, timber merchant
To: Edmundo Rocha, UNITA section chief
Date: September, 1971 (date not indicated)
Source: *Expresso*, November 17, 1979

I reply to your third letter because I understand from the content that you intend to take the matter to your leaders and you are asking me for advice.

Well I think it a good idea that you take this matter to your leaders and particularly to Dr. Savimbi so that indeed the agreement may be made in the form that I sought in my letter.

Our collaboration, whether in work or in assisting the population, together with our civil and military activities in the struggle against the common enemy, the UPA and the MPLA, can indeed be a reality as long as you want it so.

Seek then the opinion of your leaders. If they are in agreement with such collaboration, I will also attempt to give you more advice and I will attempt, should your response be positive, to be a link for cooperation in the struggle against UPA and the MPLA.

I received the 500$00 and I satisfied your request to buy the articles you asked for.

I want to tell you, however, that there is still no agreement since you still have not told me if the recommendation in my previous letter was done or not.

Since I see, however, that you have a certain interest in the agreement, and because I want to consider a person who seems to be seeing their problems as they are, and who thinks as I do and as our Government does, I am sending you 2000$00 with the carrier of the letter.

It is not alms that I am giving you but proof that I want to collaborate with you for the common good, but I repeat within the parameters that I focused on in my previous letter.

I am waiting for your reply on what was discussed with your leaders so that we may be able to continue to write.

DOCUMENT 71/5
Kind of Document: Letter
From: Edmundo Rocha, UNITA Sector Chief

To: Zeca Oliveira, timber merchant
Date: September 20, 1971
Source: *Expresso*, November 17, 1979

I thank you for your last letter that reached me safely. There are facts, however, that I cannot help considering as not normal. Your letter has no date, if this is to keep a distance or to avoid PIDE maneuvers I do not know, but for me it was very unpleasant. I did not like this detail since my colleagues may accuse me of collaborating with you who are the "TUGAS."[1]

Before getting into more sacred things I would like to explain to you who I am. I was born in Lobito.[2] I am a mestiço[3] and I stayed here by order of our leader SAVIMBI whom I admire and follow. I have many problems within the UNITA community since I am a mestiço.

My leader is not in this area since he heard that there is confusion in Cuete between UNITA and Netinho's MPLA.[4] I do not want to present you with all my problems but I have many since the uneducated blacks are afraid of my ascension which I am not seeking. I am only sorry that our leader SAVIMBI having studied in Silva Porto[5] and in Sá da Bandeira[6] is not better understood by the authorities who carry out a frightful campaign against him as if he were a communist or vile animal. I am here only because he knows what human values mean. I challenge your words of recognizing education and understanding because I do not believe that there has been a Black in the region who better understands Portuguese assimilation[7] in Africa than our ever sad SAVIMBI. I know that SAVIMBI will die misunderstood! But he knows what he thinks of the Angolan Peoples, of the difficulties of their progress and their multi-racialness. But he is so hurt by what happened that I do not know how to speak to him. But the prospects are absolutely excellent because he only laments what happened in Chilongoi and in Bundas.

1) I am not qualified to speak of everything, especially as a mestiço; the others hate me, if it were not for this rickety typewriter I use. But I know that facts that you focused on could have the approval of leader SAVIMBI, if he were not afraid of the reaction of the other leaders. If they betray Savimbi as they did in Chingoroi and in Bundas, neither I nor the other intellectuals will be alive. So be it.

2) Your proposals are interesting, if only I had the time to speak to him alone. He is far away but he always trusted me. If I can be of any use, you can count on me. SAVIMBI does not sleep and he talks about things that I do not understand but as a mulatto educated as an engineer at the University of Denver, U.S.A., I am afraid. Everything could be resolved if you were frank and loyal.

3) The mistakes made in the administration of our contacts were carried out by my colleague who was already strongly reprimanded for this.

4) Write to me when you can to see how to deal with these

intruders of UPA or the MPLA. Only the Portuguese Government lost SAVIMBI who they did not understand and who still longs for a Luso-African community that he will never see anymore.
Write to me so that I can do what is within my humble reach.
Edmundo Rocha, Chief of Sector
I received the amount 2000$00.

[1]A derogatory term for the Portuguese colonialists.
[2]Lobito is the Angolan port that serves as the principal terminus for the Benguela Railway.
[3]Mestiço: person of mixed race.
[4]The use of the diminutive "Netinho" for Agostinho Neto is probably derogatory.
[5]Silva Porto, on the central highlands of Angola, now called Kuito, the capital of the province of Bié.
[6]Sá da Bandeira, in southern Angola, now called Lubango.
[7]Assimilation was the Portuguese colonial policy by which Africans judged to be sufficiently civilized could qualify for Portuguese citizenship and, theoretically, for equal rights with white settlers.

DOCUMENT 71/6
Kind of Document: Letter
From: Edmondo Rocha, UNITA Sector Chief
To: Zeca Oliveira, timber merchant
Date: October 23, 1971
Source: *Expresso*, November 17, 1979

My Dear Friend and Sir:
I promised to send you an important letter with the confirmation of some proposals of yours that I had accepted willingly. I promised that only within 15 days could I send you such a letter. This was because I had to travel to meet with the OLD MAN.[1] Now it is done. I only hope that you will not let me down since I believe in your word even though in the war that we are in together, there is no one who has or does not have a word of honor.
The letter that I consider very important is already in my possession but I cannot send it so as not to run unnecessary risks. I want you to confirm through our Commander detached there, when I can send the letter without running a risk that it may come into the wrong hands. If it is possible that the letter reach you on Thursday, October 28, 1971, without fail then I would take the letter myself to your vicinity so that I can be sure it is delivered to you. In principle, I will be there at that date to ensure that the letter reach you. If you do not come then I will return with it and later at your convenience I will return to you.

I liked your letter and I hope it was sincere. There is, however, a fact that alarms me; the servants say that you are the Head of the PIDE that today is the DGS in Kangumbe.[2] I do not know whether it is true or not but it causes me some apprehension. If it were not for this I would have already gone there even before receiving higher authorization.

I am certain you will be satisfied with the letter from the Old Man even though he is very cautious and no one among us knows for sure what he really thinks. I only know that he is working hard to end this confusion, if he could at least find conditions worthy of that. What is incredible for him is to become an agent of GE or of FLEXAS[3] which he despises. But everything can be arranged and it is not in this letter that I am going to tell what we spoke about. I ask you not to listen to what people say, not even our man because he has illusions of grandeur and thus spoil many things that I did not tell him about. The Old Man was furious to know that the meeting failed because of Sabino's whims, who had instructions to meet with our old friend and you also happened to come. Anyway...

I ask you to arrange two boxes of 12 mm. cartridges for hunting and if you could buy me 25 goat skins and "Katsenda"—do not think that I am going to make war with lead arms at this time—acid lead and iron for soldering, and 1 camouflage suit for an average man, and for the future please tell me how much a HERMES typewriter costs. Today I am sending you two large puma skins and one small one, and I guarantee that I can send more when you want.

If you could get me a good no. 5 football of the kind that they call the strong indoor type, I would be grateful. They cost 400$00 if I am not mistaken.

I am sending 21 wax balls for sale.

I hope that you do not come up with some trick.

Cordial regards. Reply urgently.

[1]"MAIS VELHO" or "MV," used as a codeword for Jonas Savimbi.
[2]Kangumbe, or Cangumbe, the town closest to Savimbi's base area south of the Benguela Railway, about fifty miles west of Luso.
[3]Grupos Especiais (GE) and Flechas (Flexas) were special units in the Portuguese army, composed largely of African recruits.

FORÇAS ARMADAS DE ANGOLA
ZONA MILITAR LESTE
COMANDO

Nº 5297/2
Pª. 215.07

PARA, Exmo. Senhor Dr. JONAS MALHEIRO SAVIMBI

Sua Excelência o General Comandante da ZML encarrega-me de transmitir a V.Exa. as decisões que foram tomadas em relação aos assuntos do Memorandum de 25OUT72 e, também, de responder à V. carta de 25OUT72 recebida no dia 31 de me...

Antes de o fazer, quero informá-lo de que as suas homenagens pela passagem do quarto aniversário da posse de Sua Excelência o Professor MARCELO CAETANO do cargo de Presidente do Conselho de Ministros, foram transmitidas a LISBOA. Por... seu lado, Sua Excelência o General LUZ CUNHA agradece as felicitações que lhe di... rigiu pela sua nomeação para o cargo de Comandante Chefe das Forças Armadas de Angola.

1. A análise que faz da situação interna e externa dos movimentos subversivos em ANGOLA, as suas relações entre si e com os países africanos que os apoiam,foi devidamente estudada e apreciada superiormente. Como já tive ocasião de lhe transmitir, ela coincide em linha gerais com a feita por nós.

2. Concordamos que V.Exa. de que é muito útil tirar proveito das células activistas que a UNITA continua a manter na ZAMBIA, com os seguintes propósitos:

- manter a subversão mais movimentos
- fazer desacreditar este movimento;
- preparar e apoiar golpes de mão contra as bases do MPLA;
- colher informações sobre as actividades do MPLA e sobre a situação política na ZAMBIA e noutros estados africanos;
- manter pressão sobre o governo de ZAMBIA no sentido de alterar a sua políti... ca em relação à PORTUGAL.

6. O primeiro aspecto - o de manter a população numa atitude desfavorável ao MPLA - é muito importante pois quase todos os outros aspectos decorrem de... le. Por outro lado, o mal estar e o seu ambiente que se pode criar em rela... ção àquele movimento agravará, só por si, as dificuldades de fixação na... faixa zambiana e de trânsito nare território nacional.

b. Haveria muita vantagem em desacreditar aquele movimento, difundido à Verda... des que não há territórios libertados, que não escolas nem hospitais do... MPLA em ANGOLA, que a população que o segue esses terror, fome e desconfor... to, que não conquistaram nenhuma povoação e só tem tido desastre. Por gun... ta-se-lhes onde estão os chefes e os guerrilheiros conhecidos, como forem...

Document 72/8

Document 72/9

OPERATION TIMBER BECOMES OFFICIAL: NOVEMBER 1971–FEBRUARY 1972

DOCUMENT 71/7
Kind of Document: Memorandum
From: DGS, Luanda[1]
To: Governor General of Angola[2]
Date: November 10, 1971
Source: *Expresso*, November 17, 1979

For some time UNITA troops have been pursued by the MPLA and UPA. It remains in its "areas of refuge" only operating sporadically. Its strategy is directed solely for survival. The recently verified presentations of its militants, and others which are anticipated, mean that something is not normal.

In these circumstances, UNITA continues dedicated to itself with a doctrine that once made heroes and is now capable of making "traitors" [quotation marks in original].

This is what seems to be deduced from the letters, photocopies of which are enclosed, sent by a UNITA soldier to a logger from Cangumbe whose replies are also enclosed in photocopies. After emphasizing that the loggers of that region after the interruption in wood cutting returned to their activity without any reaction on the part of UNITA being verified, the content of these letters shows, apart from a situation that appears to be desperate, mainly because of the UNITA's impotence in safeguarding the population and shaking off the pressure from the MPLA which is directed toward elimination, a possibility of reconciliation and mutual understanding, including officials in their dialogue.

It is considered of great interest to increase contacts with responsible UNITA troops through Cangumbe loggers, with a view to a closer approximation, especially with Savimbi, and consequently to their possible retrieval for which we have seen efforts exerted for some time. For this purpose, we also fully considered the appropriateness of offering them some articles of primary need, not only as proof of our good intentions but also as a means of attracting them more easily to us and winning their trust.

So as to achieve such approximation and possible retrieval, a commission has been formed chaired by His Excellency the General in Command of the Eastern Military Zone[3], and consisting of the respective Chief of Staff, chiefs of the 2nd and 5th sections, and chief of the sub-delegation of the DGS in Luso. His Excellency the Governor of the district of Moxico expressed his full support.

Having explained the issue, would Your Excellency be so kind as to decide what is more advantageous according to your good judgment.

[1]The director of the DGS for Angola was Anibal de São José Lopes.
[2]The Governor-General of Angola was Lt. Col. Camilo Rebocho Vaz, who served from 1966 to 1972, when he was replaced by Fernando Santos e Castro.
[3]General Bettencourt Rodrigues.

DOCUMENT 71/8
Kind of Document: Handwritten comments on previous document
From: Governor General of Angola[1]
To: Minister of Overseas, Lisbon[2]
Date: November 22, 1971
Source: *Expresso*, November 17, 1979

1. Seen with much interest.
2. I approve all the activities already undertaken and the direction being followed with a view to contacting UNITA and the possible collaboration against UPA and MPLA.
Should the results be positive, this Government is immediately able to undertake a financial effort capable of supporting all the population under the influence of UNITA. I think it interesting to obtain, even in positive circumstances, a position "accomodating" Savimbi in order to collaborate in the above mentioned struggle and advancement of the people.
3. Dossier acknowledged and transmitted to His Excellency the Minister who is requested to give guidance. November 22, 1971.

[1]Lt. Col. Camilo Rebocho Vaz.
[2]Silva Cunha.

DOCUMENT 71/9
Kind of Document: Memorandum
From: DGS, Luanda[1]
To: Director General of Security, Lisbon[2]
Date: November 22, 1971
Source: *Expresso*, November 17, 1979

Subject: UNITA—Possible retrieval of its troops.
I have the honor to send to Your Excellency a photocopy of report
no. 68/17-D. Inf./2ndSec.[3] of November 10, 1971 and copies of the
two documents referred to therein explaining the current situation of
UNITA and possibilities of retrieving its troops, with the note that it
gave rise to from His Excellency, the Governor General, requesting
that the matter be made known to His Excellency the Minister
through Your Excellency.

[1]Anibal de São José Lopes.
[2]The national Director of the DGS was Major Fernando Silva Pais.
[3]Information Department, Second Section.

DOCUMENT 71/10
Kind of Document: Minutes of meeting
From: Working Group Timber, Luso
Date: November 30, 1971
Source: *Expresso*, November 24, 1979
Note: The following is a paraphrase of the minutes by Augusto de
Carvalho, of *Expresso* (November 24, 1979). He notes that Working
Group Timber was officially created by a document dated November
25, 1971, which was received from Luanda by the Ministry of
Overseas on the following day. Sections in quotes are those cited as
direct quotations by the *Expresso* editors. The notes in brackets are
added for clarity.—WM.

[The timber merchants reported on their meeting] with an envoy of
Jonas Malheiro Savimbi in the logging area at about 50 kilometers to
the south of Cangumbe. Knowing the region they went to the meeting
with the necessary caution, having arrived at the point agreed upon
in a vehicle carrying, apart from the motorist, the overseer and two
natives of the region. They were taken by surprise for some moments
since no one was waiting for them, they sent the overseer to take a
walk around there, and he appeared a little later bringing with him—
as they relate in a report to the Working Group—"a Black with clear
complexion dressed in a greenish khaki uniform and wearing a cap
similar to the campaign cap used by the PSPA (Public Security Police

of Angola) who said his name was Jamba." Having exchanged greetings and presentations, the loggers invited Jamba to eat and drink of the provisions they had carried with them, which he did rather parsimoniously. They then asked him what were Jonas Savimbi's intentions, and Jamba responded that he had three points to convey to them which we transcribe below:

"First—they could work freely in the Cangumbe region and the surrounding areas, no ill would befall them;

"Second—to fight the MPLA, Savimbi asked to be supplied with materials (arms and munitions);

"Third—after fighting the MPLA, integration would be considered."

Regarding the second point the woodcutters told him that perhaps it would not be possible. "Since the authorities were capable of not accepting the request." Jamba replied that if they abandoned the area the MPLA would occupy it as had already happened in 1969 in the Gago Coutinho Region, at the time of desertion of Tiago Sachilombo.[1]

Meanwhile the loggers insisted that point was difficult to accept without the third, which was integration.

Faced with the lack of agreement of the loggers, Jamba at this time declared that he then had orders to deal with integration. But the loggers replied that they could not go ahead; since their powers were designated they were not permitted to go further and they would have to go to Luso first to explain Jamba's proposals. Jamba agreed entirely, and immediately asked for them to arrange for him to receive 100 7.9-mm cartridges and some grenades.

On this point, the loggers said that they could not arrange for this material since control was rather tight but they would put the request "to the consideration of the same people who they would contact in Luso."

The loggers were not capable, however, of suitably clarifying for the Working Group the meaning of the word integration used by Jamba, who also said nothing about where they would go if they removed the garrisons from the area. The loggers added in their account of the meeting that Jamba "was always calm and without haste to leave, nor did he show any indication on the urgency of resolving the matter of integration. He remained standing, as well as one of the loggers, conversing for an hour and a half; they also said that they had the impression that Jamba had a pineapple type hand grenade in his pocket."

Jamba was identified in this same meeting through a UNITA photograph album from the 2nd Section of the Eastern Military Zone. He was Evaristo Ecolelo Congo (who was an officer in the militia of the Portuguese Army and had deserted from the BTE 522 at Luso on June 16, 1969, at this time referred to as "captain" of UNITA and Savimbi's bodyguard).[2]

In the minutes of the meeting referred to it says that "the loggers then said that the conversation changed to general subjects and they indicated to Ecolelo that life in the bush must be very difficult and that if there were integration they believed they would be able to find work and a position for everyone and an honorable position for Savimbi and it would be easier for UNITA to fight the MPLA and UPA if they were integrated into NT (Our Troops).[3] Ecolelo's calm was not disturbed and he said that if they had materials they would quickly put an end to the MPLA, and as far as the UPA is concerned, it would not be a cause of concern since the two groups that exist at the headwaters of the Munhango River would quickly and easily be defeated. Once again he clearly said that he brought instructions from Savimbi for integration adding that "UNITA does not depend on any foreign country, and at any time they could negotiate integration." This last reference was in agreement with the idea of the military leaders, who according to the minutes knew that "their leaders and especially Savimbi were saying it was preferable to become allies of the Portuguese Government than any other foreign country which would be a form of neo-colonialism."

The loggers also informed the "Working Group" that according to Ecolelo, the troops in the bush listen to the Portuguese radio broadcasts; the articles most in demand by Savimbi and by Rocha were cloth for women and khaki; he made no reference to whether the other UNITA leaders had any knowledge of these contacts; he did not ask them to keep it secret; he did not know of the attack on the loggers' vehicles in Muachimbo, nor did he recognize the name of the individual who signed the UNITA pamphlet left at the place (Lipata-Sai-Fogo).

The loggers' statements left a lot of questions unanswered and many obscure points. This is why the president of the Group dismissed them and told them that in due time they would be convened for another meeting through the DGS and they would be given more instructions to pursue the contacts. They were concerned to know to what extent there would be an agreement among the main leaders of UNITA or if everything would be Savimbi's individual intention allied to some leaders he trusted, with the purpose of "abandoning that movement and guaranteeing some relief in the situation."

On the other hand, it was decided not to supply arms to Savimbi as long as they were not clear about the UNITA leader's thought on integration and "once Ecolelo declared that UNITA intended to fight against the MPLA and UPA, they could then collaborate with Our Troops, providing UNITA guides and thus attempting to assay Savimbi's good intentions." In the meantime, in spite of not being able to accept the reinforcement of UNITA with arms and munitions . . . it was understood in that meeting, that the 100 7.9-mm cartridges could be supplied "as a sign of our good will."

With regard to further contacts, the prevailing opinion was that the place should be designated by the Portuguese authorities and not by Savimbi.

This meeting was interrupted so as to inform higher authorities and reconvened the following day, with the President of the Working Group beginning by referring to the need to recall the news supplied by the DGS according to which Savimbi would have had a meeting with the leaders of UNITA. According to the president of the Working Group, the higher authorities were of the opinion that "with regard to UNITA troops being integrated, they should be divided into two groups—the leaders and the pure guerrillas who have only undertaken military activity, and the troops that in addition to those activities committed acts of barbarism and terrorism against Our Troops and the population, which should not be accepted. The Working Group should study how to deal with the matter and ask Savimbi what he thought about how to implement integration as a base for future contacts."

In the meantime, it is recommended to always negotiate from a position of strength. It would be unacceptable to satisfy the request for arms and material, "as it is easy to understand even by Savimbi, though one may agree with granting 100 7.9-mm cartridges of domestic manufacture and from the allotment not being used in the Eastern Military Zone and regarding contacts in which representatives of the authorities participate (in this case the Working Group), only dialogue with Savimbi or with his legitimate representative(s) will be accepted. Representatives should be provided with the appropriate credentials signed by Savimbi and the place of the meeting should be indicated by the national authorities."

The next contact will, nevertheless, be made through the loggers. "Should Savimbi press for another contact and before the loggers have the replies to give, they should say that they spoke at Luso with the highest Luso authorities who showed good receptivity, stressing that the well-being of the populations under control merits great interest from them and they gave guarantees that in principle nothing bad will happen to them in contacts, hoping that there will continue to be on their part the same procedure and good faith."

The local Portuguese authorities wanted to first clarify everything regarding how Savimbi really thought so as to decide whether there should be direct contact or not.

[1]Tiago Sachilombo, one of the eleven UNITA guerrillas trained in China, gave himself up to the Portuguese at Gago Coutinho (also known as Bundas or Lumbala), in 1969.
[2]Batallion 522, stationed in Luso.
[3]"Nossas Tropas" (Our Troops), abbreviated "NT" in the text.

DOCUMENT 71/11
Kind of Document: Memorandum
From: Troop Headquarters, Luanda
To: Governor General of Angola
Date: December 3, 1971
Source: *Expresso*, November 24, 1979

Bases for proceeding with Operation Timber
With a view to giving continuity to the contacts already established with UNITA troops, we submit for the consideration of His Excellency the Governor General, the following fundamental points that will serve as guidelines to how to approach the evolution of the situation.
1) Future of Savimbi—possibility of him being given an administrative post—administrator or something else
2) Integration of the "combatant guerrillas" of UNITA in statute of irregular troops
3) Financial availability for:
—socio-cultural promotion for the people in the main population centers located within the UNITA area of refuge and who are under our control, and the people in the interior of this area under UNITA control
—The constitution of irregular troops (about 500 guerrillas)
[Handwritten note added by the Governor-General: As far as Savimbi's future appointment is concerned, it will only be possible to give him a duly remunerated semiofficial function.]

DOCUMENT 72/1
Kind of Document: Letter
From: Jonas Savimbi
To: Whom It May Concern
Date: January 7, 1972
Source: *Expresso*, November 30, 1979
Note: The following are the portions of the letter excerpted by the *Expresso* editor, who notes that the letter is "excessively long."

Once certain urgent problems which today mortgage Angola to the greediness of the world and imperialism of all colors and latitudes are settled, then we will begin the discussion on the MAJOR problem of Angola's future, its stages of growth and evolution. I only want the well-being of the people of Angola, and it is because of this that I am in the bush to make the government feel the strength of our claims. Many Angolans have already benefited from our voice which shouts in the bush. Doesn't Angola have her universities now? Didn't one walk faster than one should or foresaw? Didn't the French and the English resolve their problems with intervention of third parties? They can question the methods we use to make the strength and depth of our claims felt. That is true. But who had another alternative four years ago? We didn't, nor did anybody else. But let's not have exclusive ideas, since this Angola of ours will have to appeal to all its children and there will still be a lot left to do, unless we want to abandon Angola to the strongest and they are not the nationalists nor Portugal. This is the truth even if it is hard. If we do not manage to form a serious alliance, Portugal will always be in a far more advantageous position than any of the liberation movements. But also it will have to join with SOMEONE . . .

Even if we do not reach an agreement now, when you need me as an ally in sincere terms, you will be able to find me promptly to cooperate. . . .

One becomes very circumspect that the Portuguese foreign ministries prefer to advertise the MPLA abroad and negate the existence of UNITA here in Angola. The Portuguese government knows the game it has been playing and the objectives it wants to achieve. But in spite of the very limited means that UNITA currently has, we increasingly appeal to the power of our minds to understand what only a penetrating analysis may reveal. It is this same game of politics and of strategy. I would neither like that the Portuguese government advertise us as they did Pierre Mbala[1] because this would place us outside African nationalism and we would not be able to play an active role this century. And it is because of this that if we want to do something against those we are attempting to fight against; we will have to take very serious precautions not to allow the MPLA in the African and world arena, as the only movement struggling for the liberation of Angola before we have put them out of the Eastern Region which is the only area where this deafening propaganda is favorable to them. I have the people for this, and the iron will to carry it out, and the experience of struggles against the MPLA and UPA, as well as first hand knowledge of all the dealings of the African aeropagists[2] some of which we saw emerge so the demagogy of their speeches is neither new nor surprising to us. If what I said is of value, then discuss the details with the carrier of this letter who has all of our support and let's proceed step by step. I am confident that peace will return to the Eastern Region at least earlier than could be foreseen. . . .

UPA will still continue to exist as long as Mobutu's Congo exists, but also according to our intelligence network in the Congo and mainly in Katanga,[3] things do not seem to be going too well there. Time will tell. For the UPA it is enough to say that an inefficient and incapable man does not have allies. In Cangumbe, faced with a UPA force superior to ours, we captured arms, munitions, and we eliminated a considerable number of the enemy so that today UPA is no longer proud next to UNITA. And if it is necessary, UNITA will place more forces in the sector because for me it is an abuse that the UPA illiterates want to make war against me. Even if I were totally disarmed, I would never admit to the UPA's superiority. They are Congolese foreigners who during attacks shout—MOBUTU OIE.[4] Shame. They inappropriately wrote me a letter insulting me in kitchen Portuguese; I could do nothing else except step on it. I excused them more than five times when meeting in Bucaço[5] since I still believed that those who were with UNITA will repent. But they are not even sufficiently prepared to understand their own mistakes. With regard to the UPA I conclude by saying that in the meantime we do not need any support to put the little men in their place which is in the Congo, or Zaire—as if both names were not names for the same river. . . .

The MPLA should be given more consideration but not with that same fear of 1968 when we ourselves doubted if we could endure the clash with the Russian protégés.[6] But in Cuito our small, well-trained, and duly commanded force managed in two large attacks to instill fear where it was supposed to. And they shall not return ever again. And if those who come fresh from the fields of Kassamba in Zambia[7] return, they too will have the bitter experience that UNITA in days gone by is not the same as it is today. Finally when they attempted to come to Chilongoi, the Flechas of Mr. Antonio Mota were not necessary to drive out the intruders.[8] If you are still not informed, the carrier of this letter will be pleased to give you more precise information on the matter."

[1] Pierre Mbala was the leader of a minor party of Angolan exiles in Congo (Leopoldville), who was notable for his pro-Portuguese stance (Marcum, v. II., p. 84).

[2] An erudite word referring to Greek judges on the Areopagus, here used sarcastically.

[3] Katanga: the province of the Congo (later Zaire) that seceded under Moise Tshombe in 1960, beginning the so-called "Congo crisis." Katanga, now known as Shaba, adjoins eastern Angola, and its copper was formerly exported on the Benguela Railway.

[4] Mobutu: the ruler of Zaire. Oie is a shout of approval, equivalent to Hurrah or Viva.

[5] Bucaço: a town about 50 km north of Luso, also known as Camanongue.

[6] Conflict between UNITA and the MPLA in eastern Angola was particularly intense in early 1968. According to pro-Savimbi biographer Fred Bridgland, when Savimbi reentered Angola in mid-1968, he "set out to rebuild an organization which had virtually collapsed" (Bridgland, p. 81).

[7] Kassamba was an MPLA training and resupply camp inside Zambia, a short distance from the Angola border. It should not be confused

with Cassamba, a small town about 100 miles south of Luso inside Angola.
7Chilongoi: not identifiable on maps, but apparently this was an area near Cangamba, about 120 miles south of Luso.

DOCUMENT 72/2
Kind of Document: Letter
From: Jonas Savimbi
To: Timber merchants Duarte and Oliveira
Date: January 8, 1972
Source: *Expresso*, November 24, 1979

I only have to thank you for all the good will you have shown in the course of these long conversations that will produce anticipated results. On my part I believe that everything was done. What remains to be done depends on the authorities and whether they are willing to act on the line of thought of integration. When I received the letter of the 5th of this month my letter was already written and addressed to higher authorities. I could not, because I should not, nullify that letter nor reply further to the information in the last one, since many points in question were already discussed in my letter to Luanda. In this respect this is all that seems useful to me [to say]. We await the unfolding of events which I believe will respond to our expectations. In this letter, which is authenticated contrary to the letters that I have received from Cangumbe or from Luso (which for me are simple letters which do not commit anyone), I renew the guarantees that none of your property will be harmed within the agreements that we freely entered into. Their violation will mean reprisals from us but only when violated. My envoys have spoken very well of Mr. Oliveira. But on the other hand they have complained of the impositions and abruptness of Mr. Duarte. They are not in any way willing to go further with Mr. Duarte who has proved to be polite but with visible wile. This does not help him at all since there are no savages living in this bush much less myself. If the meeting at Luso is necessary for the sake of work, we will be willing to carry it out. But when in the letter of January 5 it is stated that the Working Group had the impression that I wanted to begin to operate, this implies my despair which is not true. In my previous contacts with PIDE1 I stated with courage that I believed in the strength of souls and not in the strength of arms. This continues to be my motto. In the meantime, I will convene my closest collaborators to debate the terms of the last letter, which will be given the greatest attention without overlooking the political implications, which for us are paramount.

You should know that a leader always has to be moderate so he can lead his men forward. When I die, since I will never be captured

by anyone, if a more extremist man follows me, even if he is finally defeated, he would have done a lot of harm. So let us be more practical and realistic. The next meeting which I believe will be crucial will have to take place in the bush again to see if the rough edges are smoothed over this time, in which case Mr. Duarte will have to be more prudent so as not to compromise what he is trying to achieve. Allow me to express my warm regards and wishes of success.
Jonas Malheiro Savimbi
Lic. in Legal and Political Sciences[2]
President of UNITA

[1] This apparently confirms previous contacts between Savimbi and PIDE in Angola, mentioned also in Document 72/3 and in a letter to the editor of *Expresso*, November 30, 1979 (see Appendix 1).
[2] Savimbi's degree, a *license* from the University of Lausanne, is roughly equivalent to a master's degree.

DOCUMENT 72/3
Kind of Document: Memorandum and Minutes
From: Director, DGS, Luanda[1]
To: Director, DGS, Lisbon[2]
Date: January 26, 1972 (date received in Lisbon)
Source: *Expresso*, November 30, 1979
Note: As excerpted by *Expresso* editor
1. In addition to the job in reference, I have the honor to inform Your Excellency that activities are proceeding with a view to retrieving UNITA troops. The Commission created for dealing with these matters has had four meetings in the period January 14 to 18, 1972, and photocopies of their minutes are enclosed.
2. Also enclosed is a photocopy of a letter from Savimbi dated January 7, 1972, appended to the minutes of the meeting of January 15 which was given a response by the above mentioned committee—photocopy appended to the minutes of the meeting of January 18.
It is evident among other things that, according to the inspector of the DGS who is a member of the Timber Working Group (TWG), "UNITA has links with Luso through its agents who come here to gather information and obtain articles of primary need and medicaments."
Furthermore, it was decided "to continue to try to obtain information on Savimbi's contact with Kaunda."[3]
In addition to the meeting of the TWG of January 14, the Armed Forces of Angola at Luso inform that UNITA "continues without significant replenishment of stocks and the morale of its guerrillas is beginning to show signs of disaggregation, manifest in deportment of active troops and people under their control." The Armed Forces that

are well informed about UNITA movements, prepared a detailed report on the movement of three columns made up of 90 guerrillas to the border region of Luso and Luanguinga with the evident purpose of holding back the MPLA and securing the link with Zambia.

In the report of the Armed Forces, it is also stated that "it is estimated that UNITA can have available about 500 guerrillas with about 250 arms of different origins." And that "recent reports say that currently this movement is struggling against shortage of munitions as a consequence of total lack of support from abroad."

Nevertheless, this same information refers "to the letter sent by Savimbi to Dr. Kuanda through Samuel Chitunda[4] (with reference to Dec. 1, 1971, Lusaka) which may be an indication or an attempt on the part Savimbi to seek support abroad before proceeding to the contacts initiated."

On January 15, 1972, TWG met again, still with the same composition, and according to the minutes "the chairman declared that the objective of the session was to be informed of a letter sent by Savimbi through the loggers in reply to a letter sent by them, in accordance with a meeting of December 28, 1971. After the above mentioned letter was handed by the inspector of DGS/Luso to the chairman and analyzed immediately, it was concluded that it was written by the typewriter recently sold to Savimbi by the loggers and with the agreement of the TWG. It is addressed 'To Whom It May Concern' and even though it is not written on paper with the UNITA stamp, it is signed by Savimbi."

Inspector Linhares[5] was asked if he knew of previous contacts between Savimbi and national authorities and also about the above mentioned letter sent by Mota, who clarified that in his opinion there was an exchange of correspondence between Savimbi and the director of the DGS, Dr. São José Lopes. Mota is the chief of the Cangamba DGS[6] post which has maintained contacts locally with Samuel Epalanca, Commander of the UNITA Camp in the Chilongoi River region.

Having reached this point, the chairman of the Working Group recommended that the contacts made through this channel be suspended so as not to harm the TWG/Savimbi links.

Inspector Linhares agreed with the request and added that "he had received with Savimbi's letter, a note sent by the loggers in which they inform that it was agreed with Savimbi's delegate that they contact each other the next time on January 24, 1972, at the same place in the bush, and that subsequent contacts will be with members of the authorities in Cangumbe, Luso, or another place to be chosen by these authorities."

Having confirmed that Savimbi had sought a link with Dr. Kaunda, it was supposed that Savimbi must have received the reply in which Kaunda must have responded negatively to the request for support for UNITA.

1Anibal de São José Lopes.
2Fernando Silva Pais.
3President Kaunda of Zambia, which had expelled Savimbi in 1967.
4Samuel Chitunda, the *nom de guerre* of Samuel Piedoso Chingunji, who became UNITA chief of staff after deserting from the Portuguese army. He died of malaria in January 1974.
5Linhares was the district director of the DGS stationed in Luso.
6Cangamba is a small town located about 120 miles due south of Luso.

DOCUMENT 72/4
Kind of Document: Letter
From: Chairman, Timber Working Group1
To: Jonas Savimbi
Date: January 23, 1972
Source: *Expresso*, November 30, 1979
Note: As excerpted by editor of *Expresso*

The chairman of the TWG establishes some fundamental rules. He begins by saying to the leader of UNITA that they are going to work with the person who Jonas Savimbi accredits and with him study a general plan "in which objectives, phases of action, and means are defined," and he emphasizes "based on this we will study specific programs which make us walk on small things to reach large ones. The military authorities consider that some basic ideas should be established soon so that we have a general direction in our work."

After several considerations the Commander of the TWG adds in his letter: "the UPA and the MPLA were well characterized in your letter. There is not a lot to add unless it is details which are of no interest here. We only repeat that the UPA as well as the MPLA have suffered serious setbacks in the last 10 months, as you must know. UNITA has benefited from these setbacks."

"On the side of the military authorities," the letter continues, "the conditions have been created to conduct the war, the tasks of information, security, and countersubversion in a coordinated way.

Therefore, we are in a position to exercise concerted military/civil action, or if you like, of war and of peace. Now, this is our main objective."

The Portuguese authorities are final on one point which is the following: "we only deal with you as a Portuguese. As a Portuguese who to date has been a rebel, leading a subversive struggle, but portuguese, just as your people are Portuguese. Nor can you be considered foreigners in this land which is Portugal, nor can we be considered foreigners in this Portuguese land of Angola, which owes a lot to its natives but owes much more to those from other

Portuguese lands who have come here to work. No one would understand it in any other way. . . . "

The other fundamental point is that according to the letter that we are referring to "we consider the people as the primary objective of our attention and work."

Consequently, the military authorities promise with regard to the population in the UNITA area of influence all possible assistance, which is not the case with "the population that is on the line of contact with the MPLA and the UPA, which still may suffer some abuses from the enemy."

The third point which is considered very important in the letter is "but what we consider implicitly accepted in view of your present good will, is the unity of authority in Angola. Within the unity of Portuguese politics, Angola is a matter of political administration."

This letter insists on "agreeing on a form of action to expel the MPLA from Eastern Region by joining our efforts in all areas. Its elimination as a combating force and as a movement of subversion can be accelerated if we have the integration of your experience."

To conclude, some recommendations are conveyed to Savimbi: "the military authorities would like, in the meantime, that you convey to your troops as soon as possible, orders to your forces:

a) Not to attack national objectives or national troops (regulars or irregulars);

b) that the group that operates in the Bié district withdraw from there;

c) that these guerrillas be transferred with those of the "Advanced Zone" to other zones facing the MPLA (called "Fire Zone") and the UPA so as to avoid their attacking your camps and populations.

The military authorities wish to know as concretely as possible, your personal aspirations and those of your guerrillas and people. They also inform that they will give orders to their troops not to attack UNITA troops nor their duly recognized camps, with the exception of the groups which because of indiscipline, operate outside the defined area except in action against the MPLA and UPA."

[1]General Bettencourt Rodrigues (sometimes spelled Bethencourt Rodrigues). It is possible that the letter was signed not by the general himself but by the secretary of the Working Group, Lt. Col. Nunes de Oliveira. See document 72/5, note 2.

DOCUMENT 72/5
Kind of Document: Letter
From: Jonas Savimbi
To: Angolan authorities[1]
Date: late January or early February, 1972

Source: *Expresso*, November, 1979
Note: Paragraph divisions added for readability—WM.

For quite some time now, we have been in contact with loggers from Cangumbe, who expressed their anxiety to resolve the problems that affect this country and its peoples. We reply with the same good will and we attempt to pursue a line for seeking possible solutions. Now that new personalities have arisen on the same horizon such as Higher Officials of the Army that were not designated for this, and a Senior Inspector of the General Security Bureau whose identity was by chance not revealed to us. The letter to which I would like to reply was signed by the Lieutenant colonel of CEM[2]. . . . Whether this is his real name or pseudonym does not surprise or frighten anyone, at least not in our ranks where this game is widely known. So be it.

What motivates me to write this is the fact that such conversations have not produced anything since there is no good will, and certain terms used in the letter of January 23, 1972, are either too explicit for me or very vague for whoever had set them down. But since it is stated that the matter is known to the senior authorities of Angola, I decided to take another step forward to seek a more understanding audience with those who have power of decision. Whether we are in agreement or not, at least the word would have reached to whom it may concern.

If we have to make some minor concessions then let it be said. But we want, however, to state that the game, for me at least, does not cease to appear like a trap. I am not sure if the men that conversed with me are capable of setting traps for me. I always said and I continue to believe that my death does not hurt me because I came to Angola voluntarily to attempt to fulfill what I believed to be my mission towards those who trust me, either because they knew me or because they had lived with me, without this giving me any claim to represent the general opinion of Angolans. He who knows his strength is stronger than he who claims to be strong.

But it was not frustration in any way that brought me to the Angolan bush. It is the will to conquer all the tides. Even among the leaders of liberation movements abroad there is no one who makes me feel inferior. On the contrary, because of my innate pride, there are even Heads of African States whose qualities as political leaders I do not recognize. But as they represent their respective countries I have to admit that they exist and govern where their countries and people gave them support. This does not mean that they should determine the future of Angola which is the land that I belong to. If they are not willing to hear my voice it is one thing, but that I should be obliged to hear the rough voice of their inside information is another. I refer to the unification of the Angolan Liberation Movements[3] whose dream always was to profit from our suffering to be in prominent places where they could never raise oneself through their own merit but through international maneuvers of the moment, which implies formidable gymnastics and acrobatics that even the heavens cannot follow their speed. Is it not so?

Having said this, I am willing to cooperate in that which is at least frank and acceptable. There is, however, a minimum number of points that have to be clarified once and for all. If this is not possible, I accept another period of struggles and privations because it can never be harder than what we have been living since 1968 until now. One says in Latin: *Deste lupuus, cornu taurus petii*—Each one makes use of the arms he has.

If there is in fact a possibility of reaching an agreement, let us see what we think, so that on the other side there is also proof of moving forward. We do not want the loggers to be put out of the scenes since it was they who constituted such a personality. *Deus ex machina.* However, I would like personalities with outstanding political ability who are able to decide war or peace, and not what I have observed which is simply incompetence and lack of deep political knowledge. If I am mistaken time will tell. There are certain far-reaching political problems that even the "delegate" who met my men was not capable of explaining, which does not only seem very slow but also very suspicious. The French say that: *La morte ne frappe pas d'un fois*— Death does not attack twice. If one dies once, that is it. . . .

First I will try to clarify certain ambiguous terms in the letter of January 23, 1972. I ask for an explanation acceptable to my intelligence because I never act through fear.

In number 6 of the first paragraph of that letter it says: "that we only deal with you as a Portuguese. A Portuguese who until now led a subversive struggle but who is portuguese, just as your people are Portuguese." I begin by lamenting and excusing the spelling of the adjective of nationality. Either the grammarians have gone backward so that you do not need a capital letter to describe nationality, or they deliberately wanted to call us portuguese and not Portuguese. Regardless of political considerations, those who write to me should know that I am no longer a political eunuch who can accept implied terms. Whoever wrote that letter should be aware of this. But it is a deplorable fact. One does not call a dog with a club in one's hand. If the dog responds then he is even more of a dog.

When it is openly and decisively stated that I am a Portuguese leading a subversive war, it is implied that I have to be subject to Portuguese law once I am with you. Since each country has its own pride in everything, I do not think that any man should underestimate the education that others had abroad. I studied in Switzerland with children of great Portuguese families whose names are irrelevant here. Science is universal, so it would be absurd to condemn me before I am in your hands because I may never appear since I understand the true interpretation of the law whether it be

Latin or Germanic. If whoever wrote it meant what I understood, the message did not fall on arid land. If it was a lapse through ignorance, then he should realize that political problems are not treated with this naivete or ignorance because hopes are pledged and good wills are committed. Whoever speaks about something must do the research to speak with authority and not use terms that are open to all interpretations. Having said this, I am not willing to exchange correspondence with anyone who does not know legal and political language.

So the Commission at Luso may deal with my emissaries but I will not reply to any of its letters because for me much was revealed below the minimum precepts of political rules. If you in fact believe that you are dealing with an agent of subversion then it is not worth continuing because I do not accept such a designation before the motives that led me to resort to such extremes are discussed. Furthermore, I have never affirmed that whites or mestiços were not Angolans or Portuguese. If you are sure of this, you are only accepting the information of the "mass media" which aim at intoxicating people inside and outside of the country but whose victories are ephemeral. If this is not reality then let us try again. All these gentlemen that have met with my men want a quick and total victory because they are totally unaware of the political context within which all litigious matters can be solved. There is no shorter nor more effective road than this one or that one.

In the previous paragraph, in number 6, one finds the following: "What means do the military authorities have? All means, the Military and the Militarized Forces, as well as other material and financial means that the Government puts at their disposal." I never wrote that the Military Authorities did not have means. How could it be since I have lived in Angola under the pressure of the Armed Forces? Is this an attempt at mystification so that the Armed Forces can teach us a lesson? It is in fact a bad intent and directly serves the purpose of the enemy when people make mistaken misinterpretations with ulterior motives.

This does not help anybody nor does a war come to an end this way because it is not the most convenient nor logical way. Many people seek to rise in society through dubious means. We may choose a path that does not seem to be the best but at least we will accept to suffer with those that have had faith and trust in us, and we shall not abandon them. It seems to me that the Luso civil and military authorities were excessively satisfied with the surrender of Augusto and Victor with their Mauzer arms. It is this premature satisfaction that led the authorities to mistakes that take time to correct. Neither of them were ever leaders that were banished from UNITA after my arrival in Angola. We only have military ranks but whether they are suitably granted or not is another matter. Augusto was in my kitchen for 15 days until I discovered that he lacked discipline and that he had stolen articles at the time of the attacks on Camacho's cars. I transferred the man to Kangumbe and he has just fled from there. I do not know Victor personally but he must be a plain soldier also. Neither of them is a sergeant. It was in fact a victory for the authorities, because apart from their arms they received valuable information. But what you have in human material are nonentities and time will tell. Wait and see.

We have been under continuous pressure from the air force, which tells us a lot. So everything that has been happening in Kangumbe and other areas are not accidents. They are prearranged plans to make us believe in the "means" that the military Authorities have. We who are in the bush measure the true value of what struggling for freedom means. But Your Excellencies, as you do not belong to the period of D. Alfonso Henriques,[4] you are not able anyway to evaluate what this means because the independence of Portugal was established centuries before you were born. Nevertheless, it is no reason to ignore the lessons of history. The Portuguese Government envisages handing Angola over to the MPLA in an extreme case before all possibilities are exhausted. And this explains the reply of the "Delegate" who tells us that Portugal has advertised the MPLA abroad since UNITA has its leader in Angola which is unprecedented. It is an explanation that puts you to sleep standing up. But it is a fact and a reality which, while appearing to be contradictory, concerns the interests of Portugal here and overseas.

But this possible outcome, corroborated with reliable information of what is happening in Lisbon and among Angolan emigrants in Paris, is a mystification.

We believe that the concomittance of circumstances that guided the existence of the UPA and the MPLA in the past (up to 1966), and later UNITA, would have benefited one or another group. Not because of this are we willing to recognize such a concomittance as a favor to UNITA, but as situated in the historical line of events when two or three movements exist without coexisting in the same country or in the same area. Through involuntary concurrence, we have often had to fight against the MPLA, for example, while your forces were also fighting the same enemy. The greatest strength and subsequently the greatest blows were struck by your forces since you have more means of detection and communication than we have. If this were the result of an agreement, it would perhaps bring for both parties better results and more satisfaction. But as this was a coincidence and as proof I must refer to July 1971 when the MPLA penetrated the areas of Chilongoi, our forces that were going to attack the MPLA were attacked by your forces on the road to the Luanginga headwaters. It is understandable because there was no tacit or informal agreement. It is in this context that we are willing to collaborate as sincerely as possible. We do not have any preconceived conditions for this. We can, however, conceive certain steps which can eventually make our collaboration a reality:

a) All operations against our areas and our people should effectively cease. We would reciprocate your acceptance to this and we would comply to the letter of this agreement. Within this spirit, our forces from both sides should respect a "status quo," which means that we would not advance nor would your forces attempt further assaults in our areas nor against our civil population. Those that desert on our part or on yours do not count since this is fated and we cannot influence such flow.

b) We could consequently establish certain areas where our forces could cooperate against preestablished objectives. In this we would be available to provide guides for enemy zones we may know about. Nevertheless, we deplore that government agents who have maintained contact with us provided us with false information on the eventual movement of the MPLA in the areas of Muangai, Saudar, Kuangurico, etc.[5] I had to immediately position patrol forces so as to avoid any information of this kind. This proved to me that it was another "false alarm" destined to frighten us so that we would surrender one Spring morning. I am used to this game of blackmail. So if this is your intention, I will never accept the information that you send to me and if the sky falls on top of us it is what we expected. This is no way to treat someone you want for an ally.

c) I would be willing to form a delegation which would be led by an outstanding personality from UNITA to hold talks with your envoys. But now we cannot accept that our men go to Luso or Kangumbe as the envoys of the Luso Commission have demanded. First we will have to effectively create trust so that we do not leave for Luso or Kangumbe with prisoners. So that in the not too distant future we accept to leave for Luso or Kangumbe, we have to hear through the radio, the press, and through authenticated letters that the government has declared a total amnesty for all who have taken up arms against the regime, and who want to become integrated into Angolan society under the declaration of His Excellency, the Enlightened Professor, Doctor Marcello Caetano, President of the Council of Ministers, regarding the implementation of Autonomy for the African Territories of Angola and Mozambique which have become States. There will be no need to mention UNITA in particular but that we would be the first to implement acceptance by joint elimination of those who refuse to accept the offer. In this context I would have many ideas since I have been struggling in the liberation movements for more than ten years now. But I will convey these ideas later when my letter receives a frank, concise, and the most sincere reply possible.

d) I propose that a period of cooperation be established to put each party's intentions to the test. I do not have any fixed period in mind. But I would accept a period stipulated by Your Excellencies as long as it is long enough for us to reduce tension, and smooth the rough edges which are still many and prominent.

e) As one of the conditions that your delegates put for our possible cooperation was the question of the Benguela Railroad, I accept it. But as a man it is difficult to accept your good faith since I was a victim of this same railroad three times in my life. My highly esteemed father served this private concession for more than 25 years.[6] He received so-called "retirement" at starvation level which he soon lost and was arrested for something about which he does not know. My father was only convicted because he was the father of someone who fought in the bush. What was done to my father will also one day, with or without me, be done to your children who, today, have nothing to do with the sense of well-being of colonialism or neo-colonialism. I am certain that if your children were old enough, they could not accept your theories on war and subversion. Therefore, to condemn someone for ideas that he does not know is fascism, which I despise, and as for me even death cannot frighten me.

f) The Portuguese government put pressure on Zambia to expel me from that territory for attacks carried out by Mwanangola[7] without my instructions. They took advantage of this economic superiority over a weak and young country to fight effectively against me. I accepted the challenge and even so UNITA has not ceased to operate in Zambia, with or without the authorization of those gentlemen about whom I have nothing more to say.

g) The MPLA receives a large sum of money from Tanganyika Concessions.[8] This is not unknown to the Portuguese government. But it is I who have to pay the check with gloomy concessions either to Zambia which the heavens do not move, or to the Portuguese government which I do not know exactly what it wants. I would like a complete explanation on this subject so that I may know why I have to or must defend an enterprise that has not only done so much harm to my organization, UNITA, but also to myself as well as my family. If it is not worth the trouble, then this problem will be the first to separate us because I do not accept what is against my ideas and interests.

To conclude this, I would like to state that we cannot become militias or any force assigned to take care of the Benguela Railroad against UPA or MPLA attacks. But we can guarantee that the sector of the Benguela Railroad that crosses our areas remains intact and for now there are provisional instructions in effect. The rest may remain under the responsibility of those who have more "military and militarized means. . . . "

I do not personally have any aspiration which is not related to the solution of the Angolan problem as a whole. I know that with our cooperation the MPLA, which is at least for the moment the only force that could give you more headaches, would be not only contained but also eliminated from the Eastern Region. Afterwards, it would be up to the government of the State of Angola to decide what to do. We do not overlook the fact that without the professors who operate here from the Metropolis and other educational institutions, Angolan intellectual life would perish. Nor do we ignore that without the economic competition from the metropolis, life in Angola would not be feasible. Why is it that those who write to us refer to these things that are imperative as if they were dealing with militia leaders or with Flechas?

I go back to the point that I do not understand why all the "mass media" of Angola and Portugal are at the service of the MPLA.[9] If they want to fight the MPLA why do they favor their arguments? And on the hand, everything to do with UNITA is silently hidden. You cannot benefit at all from our cooperation since it would be cooperating with a force without projection. I already stated that I will never leave Angola to go abroad even if it were in Africa. I have nothing more to learn out there since there was enough disillusionment in the 10 years that I was there.

I ask Your Excellencies to excuse the frank manner which does not contain any disrespect for a constituted Authority; whether we are in agreement with it or not it is still an Authority. I did not like, however, the way the above mentioned commission operated from Luso in which they sent me unauthenticated passes and almost anonymous letters without any identification as if I were interested in publishing such letters that would never be to my advantage. There are basic political and legal concepts which have to be known and respected.

Respectfully.

Jonas Malheiro Savimbi
Lic. in Legal and Political Sciences
President of UNITA

[1]*Expresso* does not give the precise wording of the heading, but the letter was clearly written to go to officials above the Timber Working Group level.
[2]Lt. Col. Armenio Nuno Ramires de Oliveira. CEM stands for Center of Military Studies.
[3]In 1972 negotiations were under way for an agreement between the FNLA and the MPLA, with the encouragement of the governments of Zaire and Congo (Brazzaville). Although a formal cooperation agreement was reached in June, it was never implemented in practice.
[4]Dom Afonso Henriques: a reference to the first King of Portugal, in the 12th century.

[5]Muangai, about 50 miles south of Luso, where UNITA was founded in March 1966; Sautar, about 110 miles northeast of Luso; Kuangarico: perhaps refers to Luangarico, northwest of Luso.

[6]Savimbi's father, Loth Savimbi, worked for the Benguela Railway from 1922 to 1949.

[7]Mwanangola, one of UNITA's first guerrilla commanders, defected to the FNLA in early 1969.

[8]Tanganyika Concessions, the principal owner of the Benguela Railway, was a mainly British-controlled firm with interests in mining in Katanga, as well as in the railway.

[9]Savimbi's complaint is that the Portuguese war communiques and press often referred to fighting against the MPLA, but rarely mentioned UNITA.

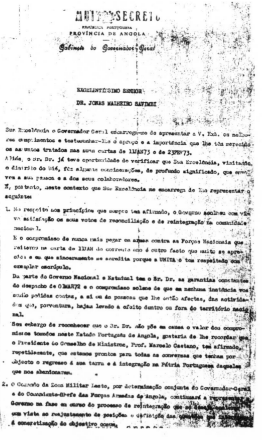

Document 73/1

OPERATION TIMBER IN PRACTICE: SEPTEMBER 1972–MAY 1973

DOCUMENT 72/6
Kind of Document: Typewritten Memorandum
From : Jonas Savimbi
To: General Luz Cunha and General Bettencourt Rodrigues
Date: September 26, 1972
Source: Photocopies of Original Document (2 pages); remainder
translated from *AfriqueAsie*, July 8, 1974, as indicated in text.

MEMORANDUM FOR
HIS EXCELLENCY GENERAL LUZ CUNHA, COMMANDER IN CHIEF
OF THE ARMED FORCES OF ANGOLA, AND FOR THE
CONSIDERATION OF GENERAL BETHENCOURT RODRIGUES,
COMMANDER OF THE EASTERN MILITARY ZONE:

YOUR EXCELLENCIES,
Before getting to practical matters, to follow up the contacts we
have been having, I would like to ask Your Excellencies to transmit
our heartfelt compliments on the occasion of the fourth anniversary
of His Excellency Marcelo Caetano's assumption of the post of
President of the Council of Ministers. We would also like to extend
our congratulations to General Luz Cunha on his nomination for the
high position of Commander in Chief of the Armed Forces of Angola.[1]
The hardships of the clandestine struggle, the realities of life in
Angola and the prospects for an equitable solution that today afflict
the people of this land, permit us to foresee the final course events
will take in Angola. Whatever be the distance we have to cover before
the final solution, we are sure that the Authorities are already in the
position of victory. This, thanks to the colossal resources which they
have and even more to the ever-increasing support of the native

people for the policy of measured reform carried out by the government. Up to that point, that is definitely clear. On our side there is only a desire to contribute decisively towards the elimination of war in this Eastern Zone, so that the gigantic task of reconstruction for general progress be carried out in peace. We have tenaciously done all within our power to weaken the forces of the enemy, although we always have to take into account innumerable limiting factors of a political or material character. Our analysis permits us to single out the MPLA as the principal obstacle on the road to PEACE, not only in the East but also in all Angolan territory. Firsthand information that we possess authorizes us to believe that the MPLA is preparing other ambushes and operations against the Armed Forces, larger attacks against UNITA, and in the same plan, ideas to dislodge UPA from the Republic of Zaire. In the present phase, the MPLA can only feed the myth of its liberated territories in Angola through the East, because of the massive uninterrupted support it has in the Republic of ZAMBIA. According to the information we recently received from outside the country, the MPLA has had great difficulties in infiltration into Cabinda. The Congolese authorities are more or less convinced that the MPLA's struggle in Cabinda will never develop, and as a result are totally engaged in persuading General Mobuto to accept the MPLA in Kinshasa by means of maneuvers to unify the MPLA and UPA.[2] The Republic of Zaire knows that the MPLA will not only dislodge its UPA protegés from the border areas with Angola, but also will give rise in short order to subversion against the Kinshasa regime itself. But the prudence of General Mobuto depends on only two factors:

a) The position that the Americans may take towards this maneuver of unification of the MPLA and UPA. But history has already amply shown us that the American policy is very variable, always acting late and only when its own interests are at stake. With the "courtship" now going on between the big powers and the OAU, no one can be sure that America won't again miscalculate when weighing up this African problem.

b) The political errors that the General may commit in Zaire which could provoke discontent in his Army which is the only force that counts in Zaire and in almost all of Africa today. It wouldn't take much, because General Mobuto's ambition might very well lead him one day to make one of these mistakes that are fatal for the weak regimes of our independent Africa.

The OAU conference in Rabat, on June 11, 1972, and the good neighbors conference in Dar-Es-Salaam on September 10, 1972, kept up the pressure on Zaire to accept the MPLA in Kinshasa by means of the same maneuvers to unify the two movements. We know very well that there are large differences between the MPLA and UPA. But on the other hand UPA is particularly looking for new acceptance in the OAU to recover from the isolation in which it has been maintained these last five years. The diplomatic force of the MPLA is much greater than that of UPA, and so one can't say categorically that UPA will be able to maintain itself outside the sphere of influence of the OAU, which is only trying to liquidate UPA and promote the MPLA. Within the same analytic perspective, we can already see what happened with the UNESCO position on Angola and we are seeing new maneuvers in the UN for the liberation movements to be accepted as observers in that world organization. This bothersome situation comes from the formal relationship between the OAU and the UN. We can understand therefore that a UN delegation has claimed to visit GUINÉ. And this maneuver won't stop there, because the same Commission is considering proposals to visit the liberated territories of the MPLA and FRELIMO.

The Dar-Es-Salaam Conference agreed to allocate parts of the territories bordering Angola, Mozambique, [and] Guiné so that the liberation movements can not only operate freely there but can also set up their administrative organizations, such as* hospitals, schools and training camps. This resolution, proposed by Zambia and Tanzania, follows the line of the Zambian government to evacuate the border zones with Angola, Mozambique, and Catema-Mulilo,[3] announced on August 18, 1972.

UNITA continues to maintain activist cells in Zambia in spite of the hostile attitude of that government towards us. We don't even get simple tolerance. But we have support among the people that gives us information about the activities of the MPLA in Zambia, about its plans against us inside the country and even of the plans of Kaunda's government which, in 1970, took part, together with the MPLA, in working out projects aimed at liquidating UNITA. These plans having failed, Kaunda resorted to barring any member of UNITA from living in or crossing the Republic of Zambia. We are nevertheless trying to reinforce even more the work of our activists in Zambia, for it would not be reasonable for us to carry out defensive war without information about the MPLA.

The latest plot of the MPLA and of Zambia in their attempt to resolve the situation in the East, which is so important to them, was to send us without approval a journalist named Josephat Kachoto. [. . .]

We received Kachoto in the best way possible. [. . .] Before this visit it was already our intention to weaken the MPLA, inside the country, with hard blows but also to undermine its authority outside the country so that the world might even begin to question the existence of the movement. But we haven't been able to go very far because we don't have much in the way of material resources. But

---

*Balance of letter translated from the French (*AfriqueAsie*, July 8, 1974).

[. . .] option the best plans are those that use a dozen brave men to undertake great schemes.

We suspect Kachoto of being a member of the Zambian CIB,[4] but [. . .] he has allowed us valuable information on the political situation in Zambia. While he is neither very intelligent nor very incompetent, he could be used either by his government or by us to penetrate where we haven't been able to get up to now. He has come to find out our position about eventual participation in a front with the MPLA. What is most interesting is that this same Kachoto has never mentioned UPA, nor spoken of the alliance these two movements have reached in Brazzaville and Rabat. [. . .]

Our position is irreversible. We are no longer interested in the OAU nor in present-day Zambia and even less in alliances with the MPLA. If certain aspects of the politics of UNITA are not yet sufficiently clear for the authorities of Angola and the [Portuguese] nation, there is one irrefutable fact: we have actively taken part in weakening the MPLA in certain eastern regions. And that we can have no illusions of any kind of alliance with the men who are fighting us and whom we fight without any letup. Whatever be the intentions of the government [. . .], we will not entertain the illusion of taking up arms against the authorities. We will use them thoroughly so that one day the MPLA will be forced to abandon the East.

Peace in the East, in our opinion, should take into account, among others, the following factors:

a) The weakening, up to the liquidation, of the forces of the MPLA inside Angola. This task can be accomplished by the combined efforts of the armed forces, militia, and UNITA.

b) The liquidation of the MPLA's camps in the border regions of Angola and Zambia. This can be more easily carried out by UNITA since we have no political status which would make possible an international legal case [. . . .] Our plans have already passed the preliminary stage. [. . .]

c) To discredit the MPLA [. . .] It is the OAU itself that we are aiming at here, at least as far as it concerns liberation movements. Once the MPLA is weakened or liquidated in the East, the road to greater prospects will open up for us.

We thank you profusely for the unofficial note of the Portuguese government of July 4, 1972. UNITA will try to reach an agreement with the Moxico authorities to facilitate this transit of persons between UNITA regions and posts without the people running unnecessary risks. With a document recognized by both sides, the people who have returned to [Portuguese] posts can come get their foodstuffs they left in the forest, provided that they did not commit reprehensible acts when they were in the forest. [. . .]

I still maintain today my philosophy, that the surrender *en masse* of our people and their leaders can only be a partial aspect of the solution to the problems that seriously affect peace in Angola. For me, it is the existence of a force which can combat those who cause us all these horrors, that can operate on all levels without limitations imposed by international law, which can be very useful to the government of the nation in the long term. Our network of information abroad is large, and we can take advantage of this apparatus for the struggle against the MPLA not only with arms in hand but also on the diplomatic level, from which comes all their support and all the mystification. I would very much want this aspect to be closely studied by the local and national authorities in order to see in what measure our efforts could be of public use. [...]

There is no one better to combat a subtle enemy like the MPLA, supported by a whole range of forces, who knows better the enemy and precisely where his energies come from. No one will be better placed than us to know with 80% of probability what is happening in the OAU, in Zambia, in Tanzania, in the MPLA, once all the members of UNITA have rejoined our ranks. Tati, Rafael Barbosa, Okavandana,[5] and others have made a valuable contribution in the work of demystifying the leaders of the liberation movements. But the subversion on our frontiers continues. Peace has not yet returned. [...]

The powers covet the riches of Angola and its key geographic and strategic position, and they expect the ripening of the Angolan situation in the sense of deterioration. [...] We can accelerate the ripening inside the liberation movements and in the camp of their leaders. [...] Although I have gone on at length about the MPLA, we cannot fail to recognize that it is no more a seven-headed monster which we cannot attack. If I don't say more about UPA, it is because I don't think UPA has a future as a serious enemy in the present situation. Moreover, the information we have about UPA is more fragmentary, because it is only by way of Katanga that we can get more or less serious information. [...]

That said, UNITA requests from Your Excellencies a temporary authorization to use the corridor between the Lufuta-Luanguinga and Luanguinga-Luvo rivers. The authorities know that we have a mobile force on the banks on the Luanguinga, near the border with Zambia. It is this force, in April and May, that attacked the MPLA in Zambia and forced them out of Lutembo.[6] But these forces run the danger of being attacked by the militia in Lutembo. But they have instructions never to return fire from the militia in the case of an unexpected encounter, but to retreat as quickly as possible and to notify me.

The MPLA bases that we have located are the following:

1) Mushukula, with 20 guerrillas armed with rifles and PPx's; Lioko, with 15 persons armed with PPx's and one light machine gun; Muanamunguela, with 10 permanent elements armed with rifles, Chinese machine guns and a rocket-launcher (this camp sometimes

houses more than 30 people), which have in mind an operation against UNITA or reinforcement of their zones in Quembo [....] This is also where "Angola Livre" is stationed, who in Zambia moves between the bases at Cassamba and Nguvu.

2) There are other camps at Nguvu, with 20 guerrillas armed with PPx's, P.M.'s, and hand-grenades. This camp also has a field hospital under the direction of Dr. Eduardo dos Santos; Litapi, with effectives of between 10 and 15 persons armed mainly with Mausers and P.M.'s. This camp has the objective of setting up liaison with Cassamba, Chavuma, and Balovale.

On the Kalabo line towards the border with Cuando-Cubango one finds several camps of which the best known is that of Shikongo, which has at least 50 persons armed with the MPLA's usual weapons, a military instructor, a doctor and several nurses, three teachers, and where they are going to build a school with aid from Denmark. Three of our soldiers captured at Kalabo have been sent there for training, but fled from Shikongo with their weapons, on September 5, and are on the way to my base. It is they who gave is this information and also the fact that we have had the possibility of sending some of our men, disguised as MPLA members, to attend meetings organized by Chipenda and another MPLA leader. Daniel Chipenda has already left Shikongo, but a mestizo has arrived who according to the description must be Carreira or Jorge but who is called Diaquite.

On the Mungu-Senanga line there are two better-known camps: Nangweshi and Sangombo. [...]

The operations we have undertaken against the MPLA have been the greatest success. Our forces which operate in the Quembo sector, between the Cassingo and Micosso rivers, from July 28, 1972 and August 15, 1972, have had the following results: [...]

[Note by *AfriqueAsie* editors—There follows a list of operations undertaken against the MPLA and arms and ammunition supposedly taken during combat or found in caches.]

As far as the region indicated in your letter of September 16, 1972, ref. 2851/2, a group of 50 persons was sent there to see what was happening in this UNITA sector, already occupied by our men, according to my instructions. I have not yet received any further information on the subject.

With reference to providing guides, our position remains the same. We are ready to provide you with them, as soon as a camp has been positively located. The difficulty comes from the fact that the enemy finds footprints of our men after they withdraw. We have therefore adopted the method of sending a group with the mission of immediately attacking the camp that is localized. We believe that what would facilitate the mission of the guides would be joint operations between our troops and yours in a predetermined sector. The problem should be studied with our delegation so that we can then determine the preparations necessary for such an operation. In connection with that which I have explained to you about sending a group to the Munhango river region, I would like to get authorization to send patrols to the North and South of the Benguela Railway in the region bounded by Kangumbe, Kachipoque, and Slaenu, in order to uncover possible movements of UPA and avoid that in the future UPA elements commit other acts of sabotage which can be attributed to UNITA. [...] We are counting on setting up an armed group on the other side of the Mucanda river in the direction of Kangumbe to block UPA [...] from attacking the forces stationed at Kangumbe or even the timber merchants, which would put our correspondence in danger. [...]

With respect to your letter of July 20, 1972, ref. 1457/2, we need to begin to implement the first phases of the support which the national authorities can furnish to UNITA. On a trial basis, we would like to receive:

[Note by *AfriqueAsie* editors—Savimbi gives a list, ranging from seeds to cattle, "which can be sent on loan basis," to school supplies (in much detail), medical supplies and medicines.]

When we have sick people who need more specialized medical care, we will send them towards Kangumbe so that our timber merchant friends can send them to Luso or so that they can receive care there. [...]

If there are points I have forgotten, I ask you to mention them to our delegation.

I would like to add to this memorandum, where I have tried to be as sincere as possible, a request which has special significance for me. I again request Your Excellencies to supply me with at least 1,500 cartridges of 7.62 ammunition because our actions against the MPLA and UPA always use arms of this caliber. I ask that you pay particular attention to this request because we do not use these arms against national troops. My request for hand-grenades is withdrawn because we have enough for some time.

With regard to camouflage, we will ask the timber merchants for other cloth, as you suggest. But I ask that you send me as soon as possible at least two good uniforms from good genuine camouflage cloth, one for me and one for Puna.

I forgot to speak to you about the possibility of sending fishing nets and fishhooks with several barbs so that we can take advantages of the potential of the Lungué-Bungo. The fishhooks should be large and not narrow because at this season there are only large fish. And, with the medicine, could you also send some syringes [...?]

I beg Your Excellencies to accept my expression of high esteem,

Lungué-Bungo, 26 September 1972
JONAS MALHEIRO SAVIMBI
Lic. in Political and Legal Studies,
University of Lausanne,
President of UNITA

[1]General Joaquim da Luz Cunha, who replaced General Costa Gomes in 1972.

[2]For more background on the MPLA/FNLA negotiations, see Marcum, v. II, pp. 206-210.

[3]Catema-Mulilo (also Katima-Mulilo), in southwestern Zambia on the border with Namibia's Caprivi strip.

[4]CIB: Central Intelligence Bureau.

[5]Alexandre Taty (Tati) was minister of armaments for Holden Roberto's FNLA when he defected to the Portuguese after secret contacts with PIDE. From the province of Cabinda, he later collaborated with Portuguese counterinsurgency efforts there. Rafael Barbosa was a leader of the PAIGC in Guinea-Bissau who defected to the Portuguese, while Okavandana (sic) is probably Savimbi's spelling of Nkavandame, a leader of FRELIMO in Mozambique who defected to the Portuguese and was implicated in the plots leading up to the assassination of FRELIMO's first president, Eduardo Mondlane.

[6]Lutembo, about 50 miles from the Zambian border and roughly 150 miles southeast of Luso.

DOCUMENT 72/7
Kind of Document: Typewritten Letter
From: Jonas Savimbi
To: Lt. Col. Arménio Nuno Ramires de Oliveira
Date: October 25, 1972
Source: Photocopies of original document (3 pages)

THE DISTINGUISHED ARMENIO NUNO RAMIRES DE OLIVEIRA
LT. COL. OF THE C. E. M.
CHIEF OF STAFF, EASTERN MILITARY ZONE

LUSO

A few days ago I asked our Captain Clemente[1] to send a note to Your Excellency to thank you for the delivery of the 7.62-caliber ammunition and also to express our satisfaction that each meeting has taken us closer to the larger objectives which we all want to reach. With this letter I am sending the duplicate of your note no. 3081/2 of September 30, 1972, properly signed as it stipulated in the upper right-hand corner of the same note.

An action against the UPA men has already been carried out on October 12, 1972, which gave us the following results: 6 weapons captured, all PM baretta, five anti-personnel mines, 3 60-mm mortar shells, 250 cartridges of various calibers, and a variety of uniforms. As soon as the camp referred to in the two notes Your Excellency had the kindness to send me was located, we found out that the UPA men had moved. In order not to lose time, our combat group pursued them, finding them at SUTA, at a brook called IMONOMONO which is a tributary of the CASSAI river. But as we knew that they had had many contacts with the people living in the area, our combat groups continue in the area and I will instruct them to stay there until the end of November to see if we can obtain greater results even up to destroying their infrastructures. This is included in area 1.

On October 13, 1972, our forces carried out an operation against the men of MPLA. A group made up of 20 men, with only 17 of them armed, had infiltrated into our areas without us being able to meet up with them. After they had carried out their usual insubordinations, they retreated in the direction of Quembo. For this reason I didn't get time to inform the COMMAND of the Eastern Military Zone. So our men had to follow the IN[2] up to CASSINGO. We found them dancing "MAKOPO" and violently attacked them. The operation gave the following results: 1 Chinese PM, 1 PM 44, one 44-mm rocket-launcher with two shells, 15 Chinese-type grenades with wooden handles, 185 rifle rounds, tents, and various uniforms. Our men got the information that there were in the same area three more enemy camps at the rivers CARILONGUE, LUELA and finally in CHISSIMBA. Each one of these camps has no more than 20 guerrillas. Therefore we ask his Excellency the General in Command of the Eastern Military Zone for permission for our forces to act in areas 2 and 3 from November 5, 1972, for a period of one month at the maximum or until an action is carried out, for our forces to leave immediately afterwards.

Some months ago we captured a 7.92-caliber machine gun from the UPA men. At present the weapon doesn't work well, the major problem being that it cuts the cases when they are extracted. I ask Your Excellency if there might be the possibility of sending it over there to be repaired, since it is a weapon we have great lack of.

Also I remind Your Excellency that through our Captain Clemente I made an urgent request for the return of an individual who answers to the name Baptista SASSALA, of Ganjize, whose brother is the bossman of Mr. Oliveira. That individual is implicated in the formation of UPA cells in UNITA areas. He has been working at this for some time, but only now was it possible for us to detect his trick. It would be a great advantage to have him here so as to dismantle the network completely. Some of his accomplices are already detained but we can't advance any further because everyone simply fingers SASSALA as the one who was leading the operations, and therefore the only one to know the others. We guarantee that we would return him if the Authorities think it necessary.

I have in my possession an OAU document which I consider of great importance. It just came to my hands. The document deals precisely with the supply of arms to the MPLA and to other movements that act in Portuguese territories, quality, quantity, finances, means of transport, etc. I think that it is useful since it reflects the spirit that dominated the last meeting of African Heads of State in Rabat last June. As soon as I finish studying it, I will pass it on by the usual means or if there is a possibility of a more urgent meeting then our delegation will take the document because it would be a great pity if such an important document got lost.

As to the possibility of a meeting with me, I have always been willing to meet with people who are authorized to discuss orally what I think and what is the definitive position of the State and National Authorities about what we have been doing. Therefore, I do not hesitate before such a meeting which could advance things greatly. But our meeting would have to be prepared by our delegation, so that there could be a minimum of agreement about the place, the date, the means, the principal points of discussion, and the individuals to take part in the discussion. This is one more point that can be discussed in the next meeting. Once that is done, I think our delegation can already next time bring concrete proposals about the possibility of installation of a radio receiver/transmitter post near us. I can't set the next meeting simply because many points of my memorandum have not yet been studied by the high State Authorities. I hope to receive some information in this respect so that I can go further in the elaboration of my ideas.

I would like to use this occasion to send our respectful greetings to His Excellency Engineer SANTOS E CASTRO on his nomination to the high post of Governor General of Angola.

Respectfully,
Jonas Malheiro Savimbi, Lic. C.P.-J.

1This is the same person as Jamba, referred to in document 71/10.
2IN: abbreviation for inimigo (enemy).

DOCUMENT 72/8
Kind of Document: Typewritten Letter
From: Lt. Col. Ramires de Oliveira
To: Jonas Savimbi
Date: November 4, 1972
Source: Photocopy of original document (1 page); remainder translated from *AfriqueAsie*, July 8, 1974, as indicated in text.

ARMED FORCES OF ANGOLA
EASTERN MILITARY ZONE
COMMAND

No. 5297/2
Pg. 215.07

FOR the Distinguished Dr. Jonas Malheiro Savimbi

His Excellency the General, Commander of the Eastern Military Zone, has asked me to transmit to Your Excellency the decisions that were taken in relation to the subjects of your Memorandum of September 26, 1972, and, also, to respond to your letter of October 25, 1972, received on the 31st of the same month.

Before doing so, I want to inform you that your congratulations on the fourth anniversary of the assumption by His Excellency Professor MARCELO CAETANO of the post of President of the Council of Ministers, were transmitted to LISBON. For his part, His Excellency General LUZ CUNHA thanks you for the greetings directed to him on his nomination for the post of Commander-in-Chief of the Armed Forces of Angola.

1. The analysis you make of the internal and external situation of the subversive movements in ANGOLA, their relations with each other and with the African countries that support them, was carefully studied and highly appreciated. As I have already had occasion to transmit to you, it coincides in general terms with our analysis.

2. We agree with Your Excellency that it is very useful to make use of the activist cells which UNITA continues to maintain in ZAMBIA, with the following objectives:

—keep the people in an attitude unfavorable to the MPLA;

—discredit that movement;

—prepare and support attacks against MPLA bases;

—Collect information on the activities of the MPLA and about the political situation in ZAMBIA and other African states;

—maintain pressure on the ZAMBIAN government with the aim of changing its policy towards PORTUGAL.

a. The first aspect—that of maintaining the people in an attitude unfavorable to the MPLA—is very important because almost all the other aspects flow from it. On the other hand, discomfort and the bad atmosphere that one can create for that movement can aggravate, in themselves, the difficulties in Zambia and in transit to Angola.

b. There would be a great advantage in discrediting that movement, spreading the Truth: that there are no liberated territories, that there are neither schools nor hospitals of the MPLA in ANGOLA, that the people that follow them find terror, hunger, and discomfort, that they have not taken any towns and that they have only had disasters. Ask them where are the chiefs and the well-known guerrillas?* How many have been wounded among those who reached Zambia? Where are the arms? Etc.

c. The preparation and carrying out of attacks should be with the firm support of the people. The authorities would look with interest on an action against a specific objective, as we will see further on.

---

*Balance of letter translated from the French (AfriqueAsie, July 8, 1974).

d. Collecting information would be very important. Still there is the problem of their distribution. This would be a point to deal with in a next meeting.

e. The political pressure to put on the government of Zambia by specialists would also be very interesting to the extent to which it could create a different attitude, on the part of this government or another, towards the subversive movements on Zambian territory.

3. One of the informations of greatest interest for us is that which concerns the possibility of an agreement between the MPLA and UPA.

The latter movement, even if it has difficulties, possesses there in the East an advantageous position that the MPLA would like to occupy. In addition, the communications of the MPLA would be significantly improved if it had facilities in Zaire.

We know that a "national conference" of FNLA will probably take place in Kinkuzu[1] soon and, in Shikongo,[2] the first congress of the MPLA in November or Decemver 1972. It is of special interest to infiltrate especially the latter in order to know what will be discussed and decided [....]

4. The national authorities are agreed that the most important thing for UNITA is to maintain, in this situation, the region of Upper Lungué-Bungo out of the war and to strengthen secretly the cooperation with Our Troops. Therefore, in this phase, one cannot conceive a mass surrender of the people and the guerrillas. [...] We want the people to maintain themselves of their own free will in the regions they occupy. We have always suggested, in this context, a program of development with our assistance.

As far as the UNITA movement is concerned we don't speak of surrender but of "integration," as the concept may be defined in the meetings where you will participate.

We desire therefore to maintain in this way a zone of peace which will be successively enlarged as a result of a development effort among the people and cooperation against the guerrillas of the MPLA and UPA.

Small integration experiments can begin to be made, as completely as conditions in the East of Angola permit.

5. The secret nature of these unhappily implies (but it is a necessary evil) certain inconveniences:

a) One of the inconveniences consists in the impossibility of giving an authorization for free use of the corridor between the Lufuta-Luanguinga and Luanguinga-Luvo rivers. Each time that the corridor is used, it is necessary to inform the Command, so that we can remove Our Troops from the area under some pretext. Without that it is impossible to assure your safety in using the corridor.

b) In the same way, Zones 1, 2, 3, 4 and 5 should not be used without a prior request or, in case of extreme urgency, an immediate notice. UNITA carried out actions on October 12 against UPA in Zone 1 and only informed us on October 21. It carried out another in Zone 2 which has been communicated to us only now. As these are zones where Our Troops go frequently, at times with helicopters, the risks your forces run are clear.

c) Still because of the secrecy, it has become very difficult to exchange prisoners, if there is still any possibility of them being released [....] This is the case with Baptista Sassala, who was a prisoner of DGS when we located him. We have been able to direct a supplementary interrogation according to your instructions. He had nothing of interest to say about the subject; he claimed that he was the victim of a plot. [...]

6. We are of the opinion that the destruction of MPLA bases outside the country is of utmost importance.

But we also think that it should be done with some guarantee of success and with all the necessary precautions so as not to implicate the National Authorities.

If that is convenient for you, at the next meeting we can set an objective and lay out the details necessary for its implementation. Including the support that we could furnish you.

7. Your forces can operate in Zones 2 and 3 up to the end of November. They should not leave the limits of these zones because military operations are planned to the South, notably near Luela and Carilongue rivers. I take the opportunity to transmit our congratulations for the results achieved against the common enemy.

8. With respect to the support to give to the people, that has already been furnished or is being arranged: medicines, seeds and animals; books and school supplies [...] Everything will be delivered through Duarte and Oliveira, the timber merchants.

9. His Excellency, the General in command, has authorized the repair of your machine gun, requested in your letter of October 23, 1972. It should be sent via the same merchants, if possible dismounted and packaged. They will deliver it in their turn to the commander of the company at Cangumbe with the message that he should send it to the 2nd Section of the Eastern Military Zone.

10. It would be very useful for you to lend us the OAU document which you referred to [...], which will be photocopied and returned immediately.

11. We are in agreement to study with your delegation the details of a meeting with you.

As usual, you should suggest the date of the meeting. The principal points on the agenda could be the following: a) action of UNITA against the MPLA and UPA inside the country; b) action of the activist cells of UNITA in Zambia; c) usage of the Luanguinga corridor by UNITA; d) attack by UNITA on MPLA bases outside the country; e) installation of a radio receiver/transmitter with you; f) assistance

needed by the people in Lungué-Bungo; g) procedure to adopt for
exchange of information.
  12. Before ending this letter, we have received the request of
Captain Clemente, of UNITA, concerning a medical visit for you. We
hope it is nothing serious but His Excellency the General has asked
me to renew our firm guarantees concerning your safety, whatever be
the situation necessary for your complete recovery.
  13. The greeting that you sent to the Governor General of Angola,
Engineer Santos e Castro, will be transmitted.

For the good of the Nation,
Chief of Staff
Arménio Nuno Ramires de Oliveira

Lt.-Col. of C.E.M.

¹Kinkuzu: the FNLA military base in Zaire.
²Shikongo: in Zambia, close to the Angolan border.

DOCUMENT 72/9
Kind of Document: Typewritten Letter
From: Jonas Savimbi
To: Lt. Col. Arménio Nuno Ramires de Oliveira
Date: November 7, 1972
Source: Photocopies of original document (2 pages)

To the Distinguished
Lt. Col. CEM Armenio Nuno Ramires de Oliveira

Luso

  I hasten to respond to your kind letter of November 4, 1972, for
which I thank you.
  I request Your Excellency to transmit my most sincere apologies to
His Excellency the General in command of the Eastern Military Zone
for the inconvenience that was caused by the delay of my arrival to
the timber-cutting area of Mr. Duarte and Oliveira to consult the
doctor that His Excellency the General in command of the Eastern
Military Zone had the kindness to put at my disposition.
  I asked our Captain Clemente to transmit via Captain Alexandre of
Cangumbe my apologies to the Command of the Eastern Military
Zone and to explain the unavoidable reasons that prevented me from
getting to the agreed location.
  By means of this letter I again explain what happened. Having
fallen seriously ill I asked if it was possible for the Command of the
Eastern Military Zone to send me a clinician specialized in diseases
of the heart and kidney. We set Nov. 7 for the meeting, presuming
that my health would improve in order to be able to walk from here to

Cangumbe. But on the contrary I became even sicker and made the trip impossible. There was the suggestion of being taken by stretcher to the agreed location, but the secret character of our meetings made this impossible. So there was no other alternative than to send an urgent message for the doctor not to come until I could travel on my own feet. It also rained so that everything came together to worsen the whole situation that was already precarious. Therefore once again I ask His Excellency the General in command of the Eastern Military Zone to forgive me this disappointment that was totally beyond my material possibilities to overcome.

I want to affirm once again and firmly that our intention is to help and to cooperate honestly in the reestablishment of PEACE in Angola and more precisely in the East where our participation can be more effective.

Already, I believe we have passed the period in which there can be suspicions from one side or the other of ambushes in meetings of this kind. I even think that the last report that our delegation brought from Luso can form a cornerstone for the continuation of contacts at the highest level to trace out the directions we should pursue. If there should be someone who is offended by the delay that we were forced into, I hope that Your Excellency will assure him of our honesty and good faith in everything that we have done. It is not true that there are for example anybody among us who opposes the negotiations that we have carried on. The resistances are always overcome by the practicality of the results obtained and already the fruits we have received are more than a few. We can never insult His Excellency General Bethencourt Rodrigues who has done everything to help us to find a solution for such a difficult problem. Therefore no person linked to the contacts we have had will ever be molested by us, even without taking into account the security of a doctor who comes to give us free care. It was already stipulated with all possible clarity, in your letter of July 20, 1972, No. 1457/2 Pg. 215.07, the following:

"Periodic Medical Assistance by a military doctor to travel on land, using an escort, via the loggers, to a central point to be designated by you."

Therefore the question of the escort that would accompany the doctor is amply known to us and presents no problems especially because we wouldn't want anything bad to happen between Cangumbe and Luso, because we don't have forces stationed in that stretch which can occasionally allow elements of UPA to infiltrate themselves in that corridor. Your Excellency should remember one of my proposals to send to that area a small force that would guarantee the traffic of our friends Duarte and Oliveira. My proposal was not accepted but I still think that stretch of road represents a potential danger. We not only understand that the doctor has to be accompanied by a good-sized escort but also [section illegible]

I add the fact that the area doesn't have food. There are some fields on the banks of the river CHIMANYA which provide for some days for a group as numerous as we have here. Only moving into Area 1 can our group keep itself in the area for some time. Also we don't ask for more than the end of November because we are sure that UPA will not return immediately after to the same area. This was one of the factors that I explained to Your Excellency with respect to the areas conceded to UNITA. Because from CHIMANYA (area of Sachinji) our forces only can find food in KAMONO to which I will have to withdraw my forces after the operations are finished. But frankly my way of thinking is quite in disagreement with this process of movement in waves. The occupation of our area in the Sector that is allocated to us will depend effectively on a greater tolerance on the part of the Authorities in the movement of our forces in Area 1. This subject will have to be discussed with all the clarity the situation imposes. Especially since UPA with this courtship of the MPLA has already received some material from the OAU according to our quite solid information. But I will be ready to accept Your Excellency's instructions but I always put forward, without disloyalty, my point of view. My strategy is more adapted to the movement of small forces than to the large forces which Your Excellencies have.

In all the areas where UNITA has been stationed since my entrance into Angola we cultivate many fields which permits us to satisfy our needs in food without making ourselves a burden on the People. But in the areas which we had to dispute with the MPLA and with UPA there is no food, neither ours nor theirs for they never cultivate fields. But when our regular groups are sent into desert-like areas to stay, it is frankly impossible to maintain them, which causes indiscipline. The map of areas assigned to UNITA was made more in function of the global strategy of combat in the East against subversion, that taking into account the contribution that UNITA can make in the struggle against UPA and the MPLA. I accepted the situation and I haven't asked for more, but I know frankly that our part is less than in the past. But in the area of Luando, for example, the demarcation of the area was very violent. For it happened one time that our groups withdrawing from SCHINJIMBU to KAMONO near the river CHICI, were outside the UNITA areas. As a result of this fact, some days ago a group of soldiers coming from MUNHANGO attacked the people that were staying in SATANDA, killing one woman and capturing another. I didn't want to mention this to the Authorities because I only want one day those same Authorities to understand our good will to fight against this war that helps nobody and that one should find a definitive solution for all the disagreements within the spirit that His Excellency Professor Macelo Caetano has shown. But the equitable and reasonable solution for the problems of the East cannot come from Lisbon nor even from

Luanda because if strategically the policy has to come from above, tactically the lower ranks have all the obligation to find practical (tactical) solutions for local affairs.

With respect to the case of Baptista Sassala, I will accept the version of Your Excellency and I make no more mention of the subject. I only have the pleasure to say that no one was intriguing against him but he was really responsible for the cells of UPA in our area. He went in 1970 to MULALO (Cangumbe) with five other persons to set up contact with elements of UPA. Would he really know nothing about the activities of a certain KANGONGA who went to Congo with Mwanangola and who later we captured? Also I am happy to say that this week we captured two elements of UPA who had been hiding in the forests of SANALOWA and SAKASSALA for more than 4 months. Even for the case of SASSALA we accept with the same spirit the decision of Your Excellency and just hope there was no mistake; we're not interested in the case anymore.

We are grateful for the kindness of His Excellency General in command of the Eastern Military Zone for having authorized the repair of our machine gun which has already been sent to Cangumbe.

With my most sincere greetings of high respect for His Excellency General in command of the Eastern Military Zone I finish by signing myself the very grateful

Jonas Malheiro Savimbi
Lic. in Political and Judicial Sciences

DOCUMENT 72/10
Kind of Document: Typewritten Official Letter
From: DGS Director, Luanda
To: DGS Director General, Lisbon
Date: December 5, 1972
Source: Photocopy of original document (one page)

Security Directorate
Delegation in Angola
TOP SECRET
No. 299/72-D.Inf./2nd Sec.
To the Distinguished Director General of Security, LISBON

Subject: UNITA, possible recuperation of its members
References: Top Secret official letter 297/72-D.Inf./2nd Sec., of December 4, 1972, of this Delegation

1. In addition to the official letter referred to, I have the honor to inform Your Excellency that on December 2 there took place the

examination of SAVIMBI by a military doctor, who travelled for this purpose to the bush, accompanied by other soldiers and by the logger ANTONIO FERNANDES DUARTE.

2. The meeting took place without incident. According to the logger, SAVIMBI showed himself optimistic and with the will to resolve the situation quickly. He expressed the desire to spend Christmas at his home in CANGUMBE. DUARTE is of the opinion that it would be a good opportunity for the units that are part of the TIMBER WORKING GROUP to contact him, because he showed an interest in closer contacts, his wish to spend Christmas in CANGUMBE being an effort to make contact with the authorities, so much that he asked [Duarte] what units made up the working commission and expressed his astonishment that no one was ready to advance toward resolving the situation.

3. I take this opportunity to present to Your Excellency my best compliments.

FOR THE GOOD OF THE NATION
The Director
[signature illegible]

Luanda, December 5, 1972

DOCUMENT 73/1

Kind of Document: Typewritten Letter
From: João Nolasco Totta, Chief of Staff, Governor-General's Office
To: Jonas Savimbi
Date: May 23, 1973
Source: Photocopy of original document

TOP SECRET

Republic of Portugal
Province of Angola
Office of the Governor General

To the Distinguished
Dr. Jonas Malheiro Savimbi

His Excellency the Governor General asks me to present to Your Excellency his best compliments and to communicate to you the appreciation and the importance which the subjects dealt with in your letters of January 11, 1973, and February 23, 1973 have received.

In any case, you have already had the opportunity to verify that His Excellency, visiting the district of Bié, made some comments, of profound significance, concerning you and your associates. It is, therefore, in this context, that His Excellency asks me to communicate to you the following:

1. In line with the principle which it has always affirmed, the Government received with great satisfaction your intentions of reconciliation and of reintegration in the national community. And the commitment to never again take up arms against the National Forces which you repeat in the letter of January 11 of this year is another fact which was very much appreciated and which is sincerely believed because UNITA has respected it scrupulously.

On the part of the National and State Government you have the constant guarantee of the regulation of March 1, 1972 and the solemn commitment that in no case will an account be demanded of you or of the persons attached to you, for the activities which, perhaps, have been carried out inside or outside the country. Recognizing that you have never doubted these commitments undertaken by the Portuguese State of Angola, I would like to remind you that the President of the Council of Ministers, Professor Marcelo Caetano, has repeatedly affirmed that we are ready for talks which have as an objective the return to their homeland and the integration into the Portuguese Fatherland of those who had abandoned it.

2. The Command of the Eastern Military Zone,[1] by the Joint decision of the Governor General and the Commander-in-Chief of the Armed Forces of Angola, will continue to represent the Government in the current phase of the process of reintegration which one desires to accelerate, with a view to readjustment of positions and definition of the questions that refer to implementation of the common objective.

To facilitate this mission, I would be very grateful if you would present to that Command all the suggestions which may occur to you on the subject. Meanwhile, Your Excellency can be conscious that:

a) The reintegration into the National Community includes also all the adherents of UNITA resident abroad, leaders or activists, whom you, Dr. Savimbi, may indicate;

b) For all your members, the right to take part in official duties for which they are qualified, in conformity with the law, is recognized;

c) The active contribution for PEACE in ANGOLA, that you may continue to give us, after the completion of the reintegration process, will be much appreciated;

This said, Your Excellency may expect that we will progress with determination along the road that we have been following, so that the common Objectives be achieved with the necessary despatch, inspired by the faith that we can have on the basis of the results already in hand.

FOR THE GOOD OF THE NATION

Offices of the Governor General of Angola, in Luanda, May 23, 1973

CHIEF OF STAFF

JOAO NOLASCO TOTTA

[1]General Bettencourt Rodrigues was officially replaced as commander of the Eastern Military Zone in February 1973. However, he did not leave for his next post in Guinea Bissau until September 1973. His successor, Brigadier Barroso Hipólito, apparently took charge in mid-1973.

DOCUMENT 73/2

Kind of Document: Typewritten Directive
From: Governor General of Angola and Commander in Chief of the Armed Forces of Angola
To: Commander, Eastern Military Zone
Date: May 23, 1973
Source: Photocopy of original document

TOP SECRET

Copy No. 3
Luanda
23 May, 1973

JOINT DIRECTIVE "TIMBER"
FROM THE GOVERNOR GENERAL OF ANGOLA AND
THE COMMANDER IN CHIEF OF THE ARMED FORCES OF ANGOLA

Refs: a. Director of His Excellency the Minister of Overseas to the Governor General, concerning UNITA.
b. Report no. 69/RD, of March 28, 1973, of the DGS National (note No. 793/RB, of April 4, of the DGS National).
c. Letter, of May 23, 1973, from the Chief of Staff of the Governor General of Angola to Dr. Savimbi

1. This directive has the objective of defining the general bases on which the link with UNITA (OPERATION "TIMBER"), which has been under way, should proceed, with a view to:
a. Guarantee the collaboration of the military component of UNITA in the struggle against the Enemy, be it in National Territory or abroad;
b. Obtain the reintegration of UNITA and of the people under its control into the National Community.
2. The Commander of the Eastern Military Zone is the representative of the Governor General of Angola and of the Commander-in-Chief of the Armed Forces of Angola for all matters related to the COLLABORATION and REINTEGRATION of UNITA. For this end, he will assure the continuation of the necessary links between Dr. Savimbi, head of UNITA, or his representatives, and the Command of the Eastern Military Zone (Working Group "Timber," appointed by him).

3. The Command of the Eastern Military Zone should already:

a. Reaffirm the guarantees already given with a view to reintegration:

—getting the letter mentioned in Reference C to Dr. Savimbi;

—establishing with the latter the correspondence necessary for strengthening the connection;

—updating the safe-conduct passes held by Dr. Savimbi.

b. Continue the efforts which the former has been making, in order to create conditions which facilitate the realization of closer contacts with delegations of UNITA or with its Chief himself.

4. In the area of COLLABORATION:

a. The area where UNITA is located will not be expanded. Areas can be assigned for action against the Enemy, but only of a temporary nature and under the control and coordination of the Commander of the Eastern Military Zone.

b. Request Dr. Savimbi to indicate the aspects, in the socio-economic field and that of information inside and outside the country, in which, in the present phase, one can already take action, without affecting the desired secrecy.

c. Lay out the projected budget for the current year, for support in the socio-economic and other fields to UNITA, while it is not entirely defined how such aid should be processed in the REINTEGRATION plan.

5. In the area of REINTEGRATION:

a. It is foreseen that the reintegration of UNITA will take place in successive phases; in the first phase, UNITA should maintain itself underground, so as to be able to collaborate in the struggle against the Enemy in National Territory or develop actions abroad and to permit it to act on the international level.

b. Request Dr. Savimbi for his opinion and suggestions as to how the process of reintegration should be planned, taking into account the necessities of secrecy, inside the country and abroad, at least in the first phase.

c. At the appropriate moment the Commander of the Eastern Military Zone will be sent more detailed instructions, concerning the process of Reintegration of UNITA. One requests, nevertheless, right away, the dispatch of elements that the Command thinks should be included in the Reintegration Plan.

6. The Commander of the Eastern Military Zone will be able to propose the inclusion in the TIMBER WORKING GROUP other members that are thought necessary, although they should be restricted to the smallest number possible, for security reasons.

THE GOVERNOR GENERAL THE COMMANDER IN CHIEF
FERNANDO SANTOS E CASTRO JOAQUIM DA LUZ CUNHA

DISTRIBUTION:
Copy no. 1—Commanding General of the Eastern Military Zone
Copy no. 2—General Secretariat of National Defense
Copy no. 3—Government of Angola
Copy no. 4—Headquarters, Commander in Chief of the Armed Forces
of Angola
Copy no. 5—Headquarters, Commander in Chief of the Armed Forces
of Angola

MUITO SECRETO

EXEMPLAR nº 3
LUANDA
23MAI73

DIRECTIVA CONJUNTA "MADEIRA"

DO GOVERNADOR-GERAL DE ANGOLA E

DO COMANDANTE-CHEFE DAS FORÇAS ARMADAS DE ANGOLA

PARA COMANDANTE DA ZONA MILITAR LESTE

Referências: a. Directiva de S. Exª o Ministro do Ultramar

ao Governador-Geral, sobre a UNITA.

b. Informação nº. 69/RB, de 20MAR73, do SGDN (nota

nº. 793/RB, de 4ADR, do SGDN).

c. Carta, de 23MAI73, do Chefe da Rep. do Gab. do

Gov-Geral de Angola ao Dr. Savimbi.

1. A presente directiva tem por objectivo definir as bases gerais em que

deve prosseguir a ligação com a UNITA (OPERAÇÃO "MADEIRA"), que tem

vindo a efectivar-se, com vista a:

a. Garantir-se a colaboração da estrutura armada da UNITA na luta

contra o In, quer em TN, quer no exterior;

b. Conseguir-se a reintegração da UNITA e das populações sob o

seu controlo na Comunidade Nacional.

2. O Comandante da Zona Militar Leste é o delegado do Governador-Geral de

Angola e do Comandante-Chefe das Forças Armadas de Angola para todos os

assuntos relativos à COLABORAÇÃO e REINTEGRAÇÃO da UNITA.

Para tal, assegura a continuação das ligações necessárias entre o Dr.

Savimbi, Chefe da UNITA, ou seus delegados, e o Comando da Zona Militar

Leste (Grupo de Trabalho "Madeira", já de antecedente nomeado).

MUITO SECRETO

.../...

Document 73/2

FRICTION AND MAKING-UP: JANUARY 1974–JUNE 1974

DOCUMENT 74/1
Kind of Document: Handwritten Letter
From: Sabino Sandele, UNITA[1]
To: Zeca Oliveira, timber merchant
Date: January 8, 1974
Source: Photocopy of original document[2]

My friend Mr. Zeca,
   I received your letter of the 3rd of the month, for which I thank you.
[. . .]
   This is the answer you asked for in your letter.
   The leadership considered it an insult [. . . .]
Everything seemed in order again when before any acts, they
attacked our camp in [. . .], where the OLD MAN himself had to see
personally if it was true because he didn't believe it. After his return
when he was preparing a report about such a serious incident, they
attacked us again in Quembo, capturing everything in this area.
Afterwards they attacked the people of Cassamo and Nigelusu. The
news came from all our posts that there were preparations for an
attack on our central areas and areas bordering our posts. You
remained inaccessible, worrying us. [. . .] We stayed like this; after
taking all precautions we called yet another meeting, in which I took
part to see the [. . .]. All the leaders [. . .] We will try again another
period of negotiations with a view to integration into one force. In
spite of the attacks there has been [. . .] the person of the OLD MAN.
[. . .] The hard elements doubt that perhaps the [. . .] in Luso are really
interested in contacts with UNITA. We reviewed the qualitative
differences in our contacts in the time of General Bettencourt and
now. It was seen that UNITA now has the desire to enter directly in
contact with Luanda because we lack confidence in the actions and
dealings of Luso. Then the OLD MAN will study the situation more

and call another meeting. Things are going badly, and you should be aware of it.

The OLD MAN is looking bad because [. . .] inspired in the others. For another thing he had to bring [. . .] to the last meeting. The OLD MAN has much faith that there will be [. . . two paragraphs illegible]

The OLD MAN doesn't want us to attack civilians, [. . .] In any case, even if the war continues, we will target PIDE, troops and the police only. The order of the OLD MAN is firm.

In NHANGO, they destroyed the tractor and the shop of João Gonçalves. The OLD MAN asks you to get in touch with him and transmit his regrets.

Sabino Sandele

[1] Sabino Sandele served in 1975 as UNITA's representative on the national military commission set up after the Alvor agreement on a transitional government.

[2] The photocopy is barely legible. Unreadable portions are indicated by [. . .].

DOCUMENT 74/2
Kind of Document: Telex Message
From: DGS, Luso
To: DGS, Luanda
Date: January 10, 1974
Source: Photocopy of original document

MESSAGE NO. 74/74-D.INF.-2nd
101200JAN74   SECRET   VERY URGENT
FROM LUSO
FOR LUANDA

ADD MESSAGE 26 OF 3RD THIS MONTH AND IN CONFORMITY WITH YOUR MESSAGE 16 OF THE SAME DATE COMMA LETTER NOT SENT PERIOD HOWEVER ON OUR SUGGESTION ZECA SENT BY COLAB RATAO COMMA A LETTER OF HIS ONLY EXPRESSING HIS ASTONISHMENT AT ATTACKS CARRIED OUT BY UNITA AND ASKING IF THE FRIENDSHIP WHICH EXISTED WAS OVER PERIOD COLAB RETURNED YESTERDAY WITH LONG LETTER SABINO ADDRESSED TO ZECA WHICH FOLLOWS THIS MESSAGE TOMORROW GIVEN THAT TODAY THERE IS NO AIRPLANE PERIOD IN SUMMARY IT IMPLIES THAT HE AND THE OM [1] WERE FORCED TO COMPROMISE WITH HARDLINE LEADERS AFTER ACTIONS OF OUR FORCES AGAINST UNITA PERIOD THAT OM IS STUDYING THE POSSIBILITY OF GETTING IN DIRECT TOUCH WITH LUANDA PERIOD THAT IF THE WAR CONTINUES WILL ONLY

ATTACK PIDE COMMA OUR TROOPS AND PSP AND NEVER
CIVILIANS PERIOD GUARANTEES TO ZECA THAT BY THE ORDER
OF OM CAN CONTINUE TO MAINTAIN CONTACTS WITH HIM
BECAUSE MESSENGERS WILL ALWAYS BE RESPECTED BUT IT IS
NOT CONVENIENT FOR THE MOMENT THAT THEY CONTINUE TO
WORK IN THE AREA BECAUSE THEY ASK THEMSELVES IF THE
BRIDGES AND ROADS WORK FOR THE LOGGERS THEN CAN'T
THEY BE USED BY OUR TROOPS AGAINST THEM PERIOD EVEN
SAYS THAT CAN SEND HIM ANY LETTER THAT COMES FROM
LUSO PERIOD WITH RESPECT TO THE ATTACK IN THE NORTH ON
LOGGER JOÃO GONÇALVES AT UNGO HE SAYS THAT
COMMA THEY DESTROYED HIS TRACTOR AND SHOP COMMA OM
ASKS ZECA TO FACILITATE CONTACT WITH THAT LOGGER TO
GIVE HIM AN IMPORTANT MESSAGE PERIOD HE ALSO ASKS
THAT ZECA WRITE HIM AND THAT THE BEARER TAKE THIS
LETTER FRIDAY THAT IS TOMORROW TO THE AGREED PLACE OF
MEETING WITH COLAB PERIOD I GAVE SABINO'S LETTER TO THE
GOVERNOR OF THE DISTRICT AND I SUGGESTED IN ORDER NOT
TO LOSE CONTACT COMMA ZECA SHOULD ANSWER IN VAGUE
TERMS AND WITHOUT AUTHORITY SAYING ONLY THAT HE HAD
SENT THE LETTER TO THE GOVERNOR OF THE DISTRICT COMMA
THAT HE WAS WORRIED ABOUT THE SITUATION OF THE LOGGER
COMMA THAT HE WAS SENDING THE REQUESTED CIGARETTES
COMMA THAT HE BE ASKED TO SAY IF HE NEEDED ANYTHING
MORE AND THAT HE SUGGEST ANOTHER MEETING FOR 8 DAYS
LATER THAT IS THE 19TH PERIOD HIS EXCELLENCY AGREED
PERIOD MY OPINION IS THAT INDEPENDENTLY OF THE ACTION
OF OUR FORCES WHICH WERE DETERMINED WE SHOULD
CONTINUE TO MAINTAIN CONTACTS WHICH WILL ALWAYS BE
ABLE TO GIVE US A PICTURE OF THE INTERNAL SITUATION
PERIOD I ASK YOUR EXCELLENCY TO TRANSMIT IF MY
ORIENTATION WHICH WE HAVE BEEN FOLLOWING HAS YOUR
EXCELLENCY'S APPROVAL PERIOD END

[1] OLD MAN (Savimbi).

DOCUMENT 74/3
Kind of Document: Handwritten Letter
From: Ernesto Ferreira de Macedo, District Governor, Moxico
To: Secretary General, Luanda[1]
Date: January 10, 1974
Source: Photocopy of original document
Luso
Distinguished Secretary General,
My Esteemed Friend,

With this I am sending you the original of the letter that SABINO sent to the logger DUARTE in answer to the [illegible] that the latter delivered to him.

I gave a photocopy of this letter to the Eastern Military Zone [...].

I would like to know your opinion if I should encourage these contacts, made on a private basis between SABINO and the logger's envoy, or if, on the contrary, I should give instructions to him to avoid these contacts.

In my opinion, so long as the correspondence involves no commitment and is maintained private in this respect, I see no problem. I await your instructions.

My respectful compliments.

An embrace from your comrade and friend,

Ernesto Ferreira de Macedo

[1] Soares Carneiro, who ranked second in the Angolan government to the Governor General.

DOCUMENT 74/4
Kind of Document: Telegram
From: Governor, District of Moxico
To: Secretary General, Luanda
Date: January 10, 1974
Source: Photocopy of original document

SECRET
3/DG

ACCORDING INFORMATION DGS DUARTE HAS RECEIVED LETTER FROM SABINO, SAVIMBI'S LIEUTENANT, EXPLAINING POSITION TAKEN.

AIRPLANE OF DISTRICT GOVERNMENT GOING CANGUMBE TO GET LETTER. WILL BE SENT YOU BY FIRST TRANSPORT.

MY BEST COMPLIMENTS

GOVERNOR

DOCUMENT 74/5
Kind of Document: Handwritten Letter
From: Governor, District of Moxico
To: Secretary General, Luanda
Date: February 14, 1974
Source: Photocopy of original document

Moxico District Government
Governor's Office
Luso

Distinguished Secretary General,
My Esteemed Friend,
Arriving at the airport after a visit to Teixeira de Sousa with the provincial Agriculture Secretary I met Father Oliveira who was waiting for me to report on a contact this morning with members of UNITA.

With this I am sending you photocopies of the letter which Father Oliveira sent to the OLD MAN after the conversation with you and of that which Savimbi sent him.

With respect to the first, Father Oliveira recognized his mistake in affirming that you are the highest military authority after the Governor General.

I expressed my dismay at the affirmation in Point 5. He explained that what he intends to say, and about which he informed SABINO conveniently, was that the area will be cleared of military forces for today to permit the establishment of the contact.

With respect to today's meeting, of which he will send a more detailed report to you with his personal impressions by the next plane, there follows a very summary note about the subjects dealt with.

a. The meeting took place a little beyond (3 or 4 km) from the agreed-on place. The UNITA elements came forward more confidently than the first time. The delegation consisted of Sabino and three other elements, of which Samuel Apulanga[1] who had also taken part in the Luso meeting. There were many others in the bush to guarantee security.

b. Father Oliveira gave them the letter the photocopy of which I attach as well as the card you gave him.

c. Sabino told Father Oliveira that after the last contact he had not met personally with the OLD MAN given the situation in the area. He sent his impressions of the meeting through a messenger.

d. Sabino also said that Savimbi to give greater importance to the meeting had sent Samuel Apulanga. He also said that he was very interested in knowing what impression Father Oliveira had gathered from his meeting with Your Excellency.

e. The answer is that contained in the letter that Father Oliveira gave them, the photocopy of which I attach.

f. Father Oliveira asked him once again to spare innocents, which was promised. Concerning the attack on the vehicle of the volunteers at the pilot farm at Km 19 of the Luso-Bucaco road; they confirmed it had been carried out by a UNITA group. It seems that this group was lying in ambush the whole day waiting for a military vehicle.

g. In their turn they asked the Father that our troops act with humanity. They recognize that up to now they have not been bombed by the planes, but they made certain criticisms of the inhumane ways of the Flechas and the [. . .], especially the latter.

h. They talked about some subjects of international policy, especially related to neighboring countries, referring in negative

terms to the president of ZAIRE and to the "leaders" of other subversive movements.
    i. A new meeting was set for 15 days later, Sabino having said that Dr. Savimbi would do everything possible to be present.
    My best compliments,
    An embrace from your comrade and friend,
                                        Ernesto Ferreira de Macedo

¹This is a reference to Samuel Epalanga, later a member of UNITA's Political Bureau (1982: see James, p. 584) and chief of personnel (1984: see James, p. 586). He is also mentioned in document 72/3, as having maintained contacts with the Cangamba PIDE officer Mota.

DOCUMENT 74/6
Kind of Document: Typewritten Letter
From: Father António de Araújo Oliveira
To: Secretary General, Luanda
Date: February 15, 1974
Source: Photocopy of original document

Parish of St. Peter and St. Paul
Luso, Angola

Distinguished Secretary General,
    Respectful greetings.
    I apologize for taking your time which is so needful for the public good. It happens that in the present circumstances, after the last meeting with UNITA representatives (February 14, 1974), I thought it useful to write Your Excellency in order to expound some personal impressions and make some suggestions.
    All of this should be done in person because often the written word betrays the thought, or, at least, restricts the reach of the idea. I will try to be clear so as not to cause misunderstandings which jammed up negotiations in the past.
    1) A new meeting was set for the 28th of this month. Dr. Savimbi should show up in person "for us to proceed more rapidly" (see Savimbi's letter of February 10, 1974). He will expect some proposal from our side; we are waiting for the same thing from the other side. . . . This is the reason that I want to receive instructions on how to conduct myself on that day.
    2) A question now related with the cease-fire. Are we really interested? What are the conditions, means, and objectives of such a cease-fire? Only to create a climate propitious for serious talks?
    I understand that our side is delaying addressing this problem, waiting for the results of the present military campaign. But there is

nothing in the way of talking about the subject because the talks are still 15 days away, giving time to act based on the results of the operations under way.

3) My personal efforts, clearly shown in my letter to Dr. Savimbi of February 13, 1974, are all going towards breaking the ice and convincing them of our good will for a peaceful end to the conflict.

4) I have gone further. I spoke of the usefulness of a meeting of Your Excellency with Dr. Savimbi; in my view this is the only way to arrive at an understanding. Will I really be transmitting Your Excellency's wish in this moment?

Details about the place, date, security will be questions to deal with later.

5) I am using all my influence for UNITA to reduce the cruelty of this war. They have been gentlemen, at least up to now, in keeping the promises they have made, although they complain that the Flechas have not behaved similarly.

During the whole day of the 10th they were lying in ambush on the Luso-Henrique de Carvalho road. Many civilians passed, but they only fired on the paramilitary forces who showed up at sunset; they have spared the personnel and trucks of the loggers; they avoid harassing the civilians, such as I, who travel on the Luso-Chicala path. . . . We should think of a reciprocal gesture to the sign of humanity which, far from diminishing us, would increase confidence in us.

6) I dare to make a proposal. Would it not be possible already and while contacts continue, to bar military forces from the zone of the talks? Only a trip between the Lungué-Bungo and the Benguela Railway line, going from Chicala to Cachipoque. You would be answering the insinuations of Dr. Savimbi and including the area where Cornélio Antunes (Sabino), UNITA's principal negotiator, is now.

I beg your pardon for this freedom and frankness of opinions and suggestions. They were only dictated by my Christian desire to conciliate brothers who are at odds, and by the fully Portuguese sentiment of wanting to contribute to the pacification of our land.

Despite the length of this, I remain unsatisfied, hoping in the future to talk personally with Your Excellency. Trips to Luanda can be by TAAG,[1] in order to be more discrete and less of a burden on the budget.

Always at Your Excellency's disposition,
Respectfully,
Father António de Araújo Oliveira

[1] TAAG: the Angolan airline.

DOCUMENT 74/7
Kind of Document: Typed Report with handwritten comments
From: Headquarters, Commander-in-Chief of Armed Forces of Angola
Date: February 21, 1974
Source: Photocopy of original document

REPORT No. 19 RI
Pg. 247
2nd DEPARTMENT

SUBJECT: UNITA SITUATION

COMMENT:
1. I also think it would be of great interest the possible solution of the UNITA question, for permitting us to:
a. In the East, bigger and better possibilities of action against the MPLA and the FNLA;
b. In the North, concentration of more pressure, more effort (in the North of Angola and in Cabinda);
c. Inside the territory and on the international level, making psychological capital of the situation.
As far as I am concerned, it is necessary to verify if the OLD MAN is or is not acting in good faith; and he has to show it in all fields: linkages with international organizations, linkages with the MPLA, with CHINA, [....]

DECISION:
I agree with the comment of the Military Studies Center. Any commitment to stop or interrupt operations can only be taken if there are sufficiently concrete guarantees of the authenticity of the wish of the OLD MAN to reach an agreement. For this purpose there should, also, be set a short time period (a few weeks) and there should be defined what conditions will prevail in this period (to which the Military Studies Center refers in the final part of Point Number 2). It is also necessary to adopt adequate security measures so that UNITA doesn't use these contacts to get information.—February 25, 1974

REF:
a) Letter of FEB 10 of the OLD MAN to Father Oliveira;
b) Letter of FEB 13 of Father Oliveira to the OLD MAN;
c) Letter of Feb 14 of the GOV. DIST. MOX. to SEC GEN;
d) Letter of FEB 15 of Father Oliveira to SEC GEN.

A. SITUATION
01. After the nullification of OPERATION TIMBER—linkage of UNITA/National Authorities, undertaken by the Command of the Eastern Military Zone—decided by message 51/RO of 07JAN74 of the 3rd Dept./Headquarters of the Armed Forces of Angola, the

contacts UNITA/National Authorities were reestablished, through the civil authorities, under the direction of the Governor General of Angola (Secretary General), who has informed this Headquarters of the development of the situation.

Thus, in the sequence of relinkage—letter of "lieutenant" Sabino of 08JAN, answering a letter of 03JAN of the logger ZECA—the following took place, with respect to the contacts:

a. On 15JAN, SABINO sends two letters, one to the logger JOAO GONCALVES, concerning the action carried out by a UNITA group on the NHONGA sawmill, property of that logger, and another to the logger ZECA, trying to keep up contact.

b. On 18JAN, the logger Duarte sends a letter to the OLD MAN, affirming that he will try to set up high-level talks with the SECRETARY GENERAL OF ANGOLA.

c. On 24JAN, the OLD MAN answers the preceding letter, but directing himself to the Governor of the DISTRICT OF MOXICO.

d. On 30 JAN, there was a personal meeting, in the bush, between SABINO and Father Oliveira. This contact came as a result of the correspondence sent by Sabino and the OLD MAN to the priest, who had already (1972) had contacts with elements of UNITA.

e. On 02FEB, Father Oliveira is received by the SECRETARY GENERAL OF ANGOLA, in LUANDA, to whom he relates the results of the meeting, receiving directions for future contacts.

f. On 14FEB, there is a new contact in the bush, between Father Oliveira and a UNITA delegation composed of SABINO and three others. In this meeting the letters of references a) and b) above were received; and documents c) and d) refer to this meeting.

B. STUDY

01. The current situation of neutralization of Operation TIMBER and of reestablishment of the link UNITA/National Authorities, namely with the letter of 24JAN of the OLD MAN, was analyzed by our Report No. 12 RI, of 01FEB.

02. The contacts and exchange of correspondence subsequent to this date and mentioned in A.01.d.e.f. of the current report do not change the opinion of the DEP [Department] concerning the conclusions of the report referred to. From the documentation received, nevertheless, the following points stand out:

a. The OLD MAN maintains his interest, already shown before, in establishing "political negotiations," raising now the question of a "cease-fire," which, according to him, is only possible after defining "the goal to aim at," with the National Authorities to present the conditions.

b. The OLD MAN refers to "diplomatic immunity," of those involved in the negotiations, demanding that Our Forces not interfere with the elements of UNITA who are contacting Father Oliveira.

c. Father Oliveira, after the meeting of 14FEB, presents the following questions, which he thinks of interest to clarify with a view to preparing for the next meeting, set for 28FEB, possibly with the OLD MAN:

(1) Is a "cease-fire" of interest? What conditions, aims and means of the same?

(2) Is a meeting of the Secretary General with the OLD MAN convenient? In what way to implement it?

(3) It is proposed that Our Forces be barred from the strip contained by the Benguela Railway (in the North) and the Lungué-Bungo (to the South), going from CHICALA (East) to CACHIPOQUE (West).

03. Although the subjects contained in the previous point are essentially of a political nature, this Department thinks there is an interest that they be analyzed in coordination between the Governor-General's office and the Armed Forces Headquarters, given the implications they will have in the military field, if they are indeed considered in "negotiations." Therefore:

—With respect to the "cease fire":

It is judged that one cannot make such a situation official, because it would correspond to a tacit recognition of the movement. It is, nevertheless, our opinion that the military operations carried out by Our Forces may diminish in intensity or cease according to the course of the talks.

It is really of interest that the cease fire be realized, because the mission of the Armed Forces is peace, not violence, and the latter is only used to achieve the former. Therefore, if on the side of the OLD MAN there is a firm desire for peace, let him meet as quickly as possible with the National Authorities (we accept the Secretary General) for formulas of understanding to be found and/or discussed.

It is believed, finally, that the possibility of such a situation should be considered at the political level, not only during the visit of the General [CEMGFA] in LUANDA as after the visit of the Governor General to LISBON.

—With respect to "diplomatic immunity":

Father Oliveira's proposal (for interdicting the strip to the south of the Benguela Railway) is accepted, as of now, but for a limited time, as a sign of our good faith.

C. CONCLUSIONS

01. From the exposition of this report, the Department concludes:

a. from the neutralization of OPERATION TIMBER, the linkage UNITA/National Authorities has carried on without interference of the military, although the Armed Forces Headquarters has followed the development of the situation;

b. We continue to admit that the evolution of the dispute with

UNITA is very important for the situation of the guerrilla in the territory. An understanding would, without a doubt, be matched by an improvement in the military situation;

c. With respect to the proposals of Father Oliveira, they were analyzed in B.03 of this report;

d. That a copy of this report be sent to the Governor General with the objective of discussing, with urgency and on a solid base, the way in which this activity and its linkage with military operations should be directed.

e. The subject is submitted to higher authority.

CHIEF OF THE 2ND DEPARTMENT
Alípio Tomé Pinto,
Lt. Col., Military Studies Center

DISTRIBUTION:
Copy no. 1
Copy no. 2
Copy no. 3

COMMENTS:

1. I agree with the conclusions and with the point expressed in B.03.

2. I think that to obtain peace and the cooperation of the people controlled by the movement would be the ideal, but that the problem of contacts and negotiations is very delicate.

3. In all the attitudes of the movement and in their interpretation and utilization one shouldn't forget the eventual linkage and understandings with other movements.—22/2/74

DOCUMENT 74/8
Kind of Document: Typewritten Letter
Date: February 22, 1974
Source: Photocopy of original document (two pages)

Most Excellent Rev. Father António de Araújo Oliveira Luso
I thank you gratefully for your letter of February 13, 1974.

It is with much displeasure and sorrow that I send you this letter because I was not able to be present at the meeting which I wanted so much and which certainly would constitute a prelude to the rapid solution of the problems which now separate us from the government. But I still don't think there is reason to lose hope in a solution shortly to the problems we have put our shoulders to. In summary, these were the reasons which kept me from coming personally to meet you:

1) From February 2, 1974, the date you wrote me, our areas have been under strong attack from airlifted commandos, which make

necessary my presence to guide the defense of the people and all that is valuable to us. Also the access paths to the area where the meeting was to take place, are frequently assaulted by the same troops which doesn't give me any security to take such a trip. To make the situation worse, I am constantly on the move which makes coordination with other friends difficult, friends who would be ready to take part in the meeting and would give our talk a more representative character. I will try to contact these colleagues of mine to see how we can set up such a meeting.

2) It was quite late when our emissaries finally got in contact with me. It was precisely yesterday, February 21, 1974, when they found me to give an oral report of what had been discussed. It was physically impossible for me to consult my colleagues, take all the security measures and undertake the trip.

You don't need to be discouraged about this. I was highly impressed with all you have done to set up a favorable environment for talks. It also pleases me to see the business card of His Excellency the Secretary-General of the State of Angola. That was what was lacking when it concerned that working group in Luso, after the departure of His Excellency General Bettnecourt Rodrigues. With the group in question one never knew if Luanda was aware of our proposals and counter-proposals or not. With this channel of communication open, I believe we will move along more rapidly than one thinks.

What the military people say or think, now has no more importance for me. They are engaged in an offensive which shows characteristics of a daily escalation. The result will only be that we will go back to the point of departure. They are skeptics, and therefore they are not interested in ending the war in Angola. I understand this, because as military men and militarists they are professionals of war which we aren't. It is always desirable that the political authority exercise its force of persuasion so that the soldiers don't escalate the war because otherwise it will never end, if each side steps up after each attack. The politicians will have a difficult enough if not impossible task, which is what you would expect.

I hope that you have brought proposals for an immediate cease-fire which we will respect scrupulously which will permit opening talks at the highest levels. How can you see a UNITA messenger leave for Luso or Luanda when the war is still going on at his back? He would be considered a prisoner.

There is much to debate and we are reading to meet when the minimal conditions of security are met. We will be in contact with you by the usual channels.

Could you please get me a copy of the book of General António de Spínola. It is material we need to know. With my respectful greeting, your friend,

Jonas Malheiro Savimbi

DOCUMENT 74/9
Kind of Document: Handwritten letter
From: Governor, District of Moxico
To: Secretary-General, Luanda
Date: May 28, 1974
Source: Photocopy of original document (1 page)
Luso, May 28, 1974

Distinguished Official in Charge and My Distinguished Friend,
Two lines to tell you that the contact between Father Oliveira and the OLD MAN took place today [...] as was agreed.
The best impressions but nothing concrete for now.
I wrote to the General Commander-in-Chief to send him a letter addressed to him and to spell out a bit more the conversation that took place. In sum, to set up the desired contact, they want there to be a communique saying that we are trying to establish contacts with UNITA. You will be talking more with the General Commander-in-Chief on this subject clarifying more completely what he wishes.
With my best compliments,
accept my friendly embrace
Ernesto Ferreira de Macedo

DOCUMENT 74/10
Kind of Document: Handwritten Minutes
Date: June 14, 1974
Source: Photocopy of original document (3 pages)

Eastern Military Zone Command
[printed stationery with seal of Eastern Military Zone; no page number]

... future [...] and for the legitimation of the appearance of UNITA on the Angolan political scene.
2. In response, Dr. JONAS SAVIMBI made the following points:
a. He doesn't consider himself clear about the political framework in which the process of decolonization of ANGOLA will develop. He fears that it will not be possible with a totally democratic system in PORTUGAL, thinking that it would be preferable with a strong regime, which would have to be led by Gen. SPINOLA. Therefore he was apprehensive, when he heard Gen. SPINOLA affirm that he would hand over power, within one year, to structures legally elected by the Nation. He thought that the period of a year is too short for the development of all this process.
[inserted in margin: At this moment he himself would prefer to develop a political campaign for consolidation of the government of Gen. Spínola than for independence of Angola.]

To be able to make his decisions, he needed therefore to get these points explained clearly, by a responsible party.

b. He agrees and recognized the purity of the objectives of the Armed Forces Movement, for the outbreak of which he considers that UNITA also made its contribution, but he did not agree with the proposed referendum formula.

HEADQUARTERS
[Printed stationery with seal of army Headquarters; handwritten numbers, pages 13 and 14]

2. Definition of "status quo" areas.

For the convenience of practical application of the agreement—suspension of hostilities—areas defined during OP TIMBER were taken as a base—according to the attached map and note—having given freedom of traffic and installation in the corridor of access to Zambia (UNITA zone zero); having stressed that UNITA will assume responsibility for intelligence and control in that area, against possible MPLA infiltrations (considered very likely by Dr. SAVIMBI). Noting that when one of the UNITA captains tried to enlarge the "zone zero" area, Dr. SAVIMBI disagreed and affirmed that UNITA could not take on this responsibility, given the MPLA combat potential, namely in the NGUVU base which he said was still under control of the A. NETO faction (confirming the impressions of Armed Forces HQ and Eastern Military Zone).

It was stressed that economic activities would be permitted in the "status quo" areas and that, in the present phase, these areas would be governed by the regulation that was in effect for OP TIMBER.

Dr. SAVIMBI also took responsibility for assuring that armed groups of UNITA would not circulate outside the agreed areas, being permitted to do so without arms and in civilian clothes, it nevertheless being [. . .] to organize rallies or public meetings for UNITA propaganda, which will only be possible to do after the transition to the status of an unarmed political party.

It was also agreed that, reciprocally, the people would have free rights of transit and work in the "status quo" areas.

Finally Dr. SAVIMBI expressed his worry about probable infiltration by FNLA over the border at T. SOUSA, expressing the need to set up an intelligence group in the SANDANDO area, being agreed that UNITA would soon make a proposal on the subject to the Commander of the Eastern Military Zone through Father. [. . .]

Savimbi's aide Sabino Sandele (see Document 74/1)

Comando-Chefe das Forças Armadas em Angola

QUARTEL GENERAL

INFORMAÇÃO Nº 19 RI

Nº 247 — Data 21 FEV /74

Da: 2ª REP-MCTIÇÃO (1)

ASSUNTO: SITUAÇÃO DA UNITA

REF:

PARECER:

DESPACHO:

REFª: a) Carta de 1ªFEV do Mª do Pª Oliveira;
b) Carta de 1ªFEV do Pª Oliveira ao Mª;
c) Carta de 1ªFEV do GOV.DIST. NOª ao SEC-GERAL;
d) Carta de 1ªFEV do Pª Oliveira ao SEC-GERAL.

A. SITUAÇÃO

01. Depois da neutralização do Cª MADEIRA — ligação da UNITA/AN, conduzida pelo CAO INL — determinada pela mensagem SI/RG de 07JAN74 do CCFAA/3ª REP restabeleceram-se os contactos UNITA/AN, nomeadamente os Contactos Civis, sob orientação do G.Geral de Angola (SECRETARIADO-GERAL) que tem informado este CCFAA da evolução da situação.

Assim, e na sequência do restamento de ligação — carta do "alf." SABINO, de 09JAN, respondendo a uma carta do COJAN do madeireiro ZEDA — verifica-se o seguinte,no respeitante a contactos:

Continuação da Informação Nº 19 RI - de 21/FEV /74 - Pág. 2

a. Em 15JAN, SABINO dirige duas cartas, uma ao madeireiro JOÃO GONÇALVES, relativa à acção efectuada por um Gr da UNITA sobre a serração de NHANGA, propriedade daquele madeireiro,e outra ao madeireiro ZEDA, procurando montar o contacto.

b. Em 19JAN,o madeireiro Duarte envia carta ao M.V., afirmando que se esforçará para que sejam estabelecidas conversações a alto nível com o SEC-GERAL DE ANGOLA.

c. Em 24JAN, o M.V. responde à carta anterior, mas dirigindo-se ao Governador do DIST-MOXICO.

d. Em 30JAN, houve um contacto pessoal, na mata, entre o SABINO e o Pª.Oliveira. Este contacto surgiu na sequência de correspondência dirigida pelo Sabino e pelo M.V. ao Secandoto, que já anteriormente (1972) havia tido contactos c/elementos da UNITA.

e. Em 03FEV, o Pª Oliveira é recebido pelo SEC-GERAL DE ANGOLA, se LUANDA, a quem relata o realizado do encontro anterior,recebendo orientação para futuros contactos.

f. Em 14FEV,realiza-se novo contacto na mata, entre o Pª. Oliveira e uma delegação da UNITA composta pelo Sabino e mais 5 elementos. Neste contacto são recebidas as cartas de refª. c) e b) e a ela se referem os documentos de refª. c) e d).

B. ESTUDO

01. A situação decorrente da neutralização do Cp. MADEIRA e do restabelecimento da ligação UNITA/AN, nomeadamente da carta de 24JAN do MV, foi analisada pela Nª Info nº 12 RI, de 01FEV.

02. Os contactos e troca de correspondência processados a partir dessa data e mencionados em A.01.d.e.f. da presente informação, não alteram a opinião da REP constante das "CONCLUSÕES" da Informação atrás referida. Os documentos recebidos, salientam-se, contudo, os seguintes pontos:

Document 74/7 p. 1 and 2.

-Angola,22 de Fev.de 1974
Excelentissimo Senhor
Rev.Padre Antonio de Araujo Oliveira
LUSO

Agradeco penhoradamente a sua estimada carta de 13 de Fevereiro de 1974.

E com bastante desgosto e desolacao que lhe envio esta carta por nao poder estar presente ao encontro que eu tanto desejava e que de certeza constituiria um preludio, resolucao rapida dos problemas que nos separam hoje do governo.Nem por isso acho que haja razao para se perder esperanca numa solucao a breve trecho dos problemas a que temos xixix os nossos ombros metidos.Em suma,foram as seguintes,as razoes que me impediram de ir pessoalmente ao encontro do Meu Amigo:

1o) A partir do dia 13/2/74,data em que me escreveu, as nossas areas estao de baixo de fortes ataques de comandos aero-transportados,o que precisa da minha presenca para orientar a defesa das populacoes e de tudo quanto nos e caro.Tambem as vias de acesso a area onde o encontro deveria ter lugar,sao frequentemente investidas pelas mesmas tropas o que nao me oferece nenhuma seguranca para empreender uma tal caminhada.A agravar a situacao,eu encontro-me em constantes deslocacoes o que dificulta a coordenacao com outros amigos que de certeza estariam dispostos a participar no encontro o que emprestaria a nossa conversacao um caracter mais representativo.Vou tentar contactar esses meus colegas para vermos como se materializará um tal encontro.

2o)Foi bastante tarde quando os nossos enviados poderam,finalmente entrar em contacto comigo.Foi precisamente ontem dia 21/2/74 que eles poderam me encontrar e fazer-me um relatorio verbal de tudo quanto se discutiu.Era materialmente impossivel consultar os meus colegas.tomar todas as medidas de seguranca e empreender a caminhada.

O meu Amigo nao tem nada a desesperar com tudo isso.Fiquei altamente bem impressionado com tudo quanto ja fez no sentido de se encontrar um ambiente favoravel para a discussao.Tambem agradou-me sobremaneira ver o cartao de visita de SExa o Senhor Secretario-Geral do Estado de Angola.E o que tinha faltado quando se tratava com o tal grupo de trabalho do Luso,depois da saida de SExa o General Bettencourt Rodrigues.Com o grupo em questao nunca se sabia se sim ou nao Luanda estava ao corrente das nossas propostas e contra-propostas.Com essa via de comunicacao aberta,creio que andaremos mais rapidamente do que se pensa.

O que os meios militares dizem ou pensam,hoje para mim ja nao tem mais importancia.Eles estao lancados numa ofensiva que manifesta caracteristicas de uma verdadeira escala.Cada dia que se passa.O resultado só sera voltarmos todos para o ponto de partida.Eles sao cepticos por isso nao estao interessados a que a guerra acabe em Angola.O que eu compreendo, ppis como militares e militaristas sao profissionais da guerra o que nós nao somos.E sempre desejavel que a autoridade politica exerca a sua forca de persuasao para que os militares nao escalem a guerra porque senao nunca mais tem fim se cada lado fosse a subir mais um degrau em cada ataque.Os politicos teriam de facto a sua missao bastante dificultada senao impossibilitada.O que seria muita pena

Espero que o Senhor Padre tenha trazido propostas para um cessar-fogo imediato que nós respeitaremos escrupulosamente o que permitira a abertura das conversacoes ao nivel mais alto possivel.Como é que o Senhor Padre poderia ver um emissario da UNITA partir para o Luso ou Luanda com a guerra a sua tras?Considerar-se-ia preso.

Ha muito a debater e estamos prontos a ir ao seu encontro quando as minimas condicoes de seguranca se realizarem.Entraremos em contacto comigo por vias habituais.

S.F.F. arranjar-me um exemplar do livro do General Antonio de Spinola.E materia que nos interessa conhecer.Com os meus cumprimentos de respeito e estima,subscrevo-me amigo certo,   Jonas Malheiro Savimbi

Document 74/8 p. 1 and 2.

Appendix 1: Guide to Additional Reading

In addition to the sources cited in the footnotes, the reader interested in investigating topics mentioned in greater detail could begin with the following works.

Cherri Waters' *Angola: A Matter of Justice* (New York: Africa Committee, National Council of Churches, 1987) is an excellent recent summary (54 pages), including an extensive bibliography.

Angola under Portuguese Colonialism: A short introductory article with many useful references is W.G. Clarence-Smith, "Capital Accumulation and Class Formation in Angola," pp. 163-199 in David Birmingham and Phyllis M. Martin, eds., *History of Central Africa, Volume II* (New York: Longman, 1983). More comprehensive but not quite as up-to-date is Douglas Wheeler and René Pelissier, *Angola* (New York: Praeger, 1971).

Angolan Nationalism and the Liberation War: John Marcum's *The Angolan Revolution, Volumes I and II* (Cambridge: MIT Press, 1969, 1978) is indispensable as a reference. Basil Davidson's *In the Eye of the Storm: Angola's People* (Garden City, NY: Doubleday, 1973) is both readable and analytic, including background as well as description of his 1970 trip into MPLA areas in eastern Angola. Don Barnett and Roy Harvey, *The Revolution in Angola: MPLA, Life Histories and Documents* (Indianapolis: Bobbs-Merrill, 1972), contains invaluable life histories of several MPLA guerrillas.

On UNITA, Leon Dash's articles on his trip appeared in the *Washington Post*, December 23-26, 1973. Franz Sitte's report on his trip appeared in the *Observer* (London), April 7, 1972, as well as in his book *Flammenherd Angola* (Vienna: Verlag Kremayr and Scheriau, 1972). An article by Aquino de Bragança, "Savimbi: Itinerário de Uma Contra-Revolução (*Estudos Moçambicanos*, 2:1981, pp. 87-104), provides a summary of Operation Timber and related information. The fullest description is in R. Sotto-Maior, *História de uma Traição* (Luanda: Alvorada, 1985).

Decolonization Conflict (1974-76: The best analytic account is F.W. Heimer's *The Decolonization Conflict in Angola, 1974-*

76: *An Essay in Political Sociology* (Geneva: Institut Universitaire de Hautes Etudes Internationales, 1979). Gerald Bender's "Kissinger in Angola: Anatomy of Failure," pp. 63-144, in René Lemarchand, *American Policy in Southern Africa: The Stakes and the Stance, Second Edition* (Washington: University Press of America, 1981), is a good summary of the U.S. involvement. John Stockwell's *In Search of Enemies: An Inside Story* (New York: W.W. Norton, 1978) is an inside account. See also pp. 262-271 in William Minter, *King Solomon's Mines Revisited* (New York: Basic Books, 1986) for an overview.

Since 1976: Three books of varying lengths on South Africa's wars against its neighbors are Joseph Hanlon, *Apartheid's Second Front: South Africa's War against its Neighbors* (Harmondsworth: Penguin, 1986); Phyllis Johnson and David Martin, eds., *Destructive Engagement* (Harare: Zimbabwe Publishing House, 1986);and Joseph Hanlon, *Beggar Your Neighbors: Apartheid Power in Southern Africa* (Bloomington: Indiana University Press, 1986). Somewhat less recent is Thomas M. Callaghy, "Apartheid and Socialism: South Africa's Relations with Angola and Mozambique," in Thomas M. Callaghy, ed., *South Africa in Southern Africa: The Intensifying Vortex of Violence* (New York: Praeger, 1983).

Two books offering an overview of post-independence in Angola are Keith Somerville, *Angola: Politics, Economics and Society* (Boulder: Lynne Rienner Publishers, 1986), and Michael Wolfers and Jane Bergerol, *Angola in the Front Line* (London: Zed Press, 1983).

Appendix 2A

Source: Letter to the Editor, *Expresso*, November 30, 1979, identified by *Expresso* as "someone who was in the military forces in Angola from 1967 to 1969." It was sent to *Expresso* in response to the articles published in the issues of November 17 and November 24.

"I am informing you that if you are interested in examining this matter more in depth, you will have to go further back in time, at least to 1969 or even to the end of 1968. You cannot limit yourself to placing it in the agonizing epoch of colonialism, which could give it a circumstantial character and miss the intrinsically 'collaborationist' characteristic of this movement.

At the beginning of 1969, I do not know the exact date, I was part of a Military Force that was temporarily in Gago Coutinho, headquarters of Batalhão. We received an order to go by vehicle to a place between Gago Coutinho and Cangumbe, with Flechas as guides who, as you know, were local cannon fodder at the service of PIDE. After about 20 or 30 kilometers we stopped and set up security in the area. The MPLA actions were increasingly intense and effective throughout the Eastern Region. Two colored soldiers, I think, went into the bush. They returned about half an hour later accompanied by people in very obvious state of hardship, and some young guerrillas tattered but armed, and I remember one of them had a certain distinction. It was a UNITA detachment that had had relations with PIDE at Gago Coutinho for a long time, and which had given themselves up to fight the MPLA, which as I stated had proved to be the most organized force in the whole of the Eastern Region at that time. They got into our vehicles and at night we arrived at Gago Coutinho. Waiting for us were a major responsible for the operations in the area, Martins who was the head of the local PIDE, and a Black about 40 years old, bearded, with glasses, and a golden chain around his neck, who I learned was negotiating this strange collaboration from the UNITA side. It was he who received his fellow party members, arranged them in a semicircle, and put them to sing what I discovered was the UNITA anthem. Then we were given orders to withdraw."

Appendix 2B

In February 1981 an International Commission on the Crimes of Apartheid held hearings in Luanda, presided over by Sean McBride, a former United Nations High Commissioner for Namibia. Among the witnesses was José Ricardo Belmundo, an Angolan who served in South Africa's 32 Batallion before deserting in January 1980. Belmundo's testimony coincided with interviews in London with Trevor Edwards, a British mercenary who served in the same unit from March through December 1980.

Edwards and Belmundo, whose stories were reported in *The Guardian* (London, January 29 and February 2, 1981) and in *Africa News* (March 23, 1981), both said that their batallion regularly acted in Angola on behalf of UNITA.

Following the commission hearings in Luanda, Belmundo was interviewed by Angolan television. The following excerpts from the interview add a few details to the news stories cited above.

Interviewer: When South Africa invades Angola, what is generally the objective? Is it to attack SWAPO (South West African Peoples Organization) bases as they say?

Belmundo: South Africa, yes, makes war against SWAPO, waits for SWAPO in Namibian territory, and attacks Angola. But the objective of South Africa in attacking Angola is not only against SWAPO. South Africa's objective in this war against Angola is to advance UNITA. It is to justify to the world that UNITA really controls this part of Angolan territory. In Cuando Cubango, at the request of UNITA they operate in a certain zone. Afterwards UNITA comes in.

Interviewer: You told the Commission that there are ex-FNLA in 32 Batallion. Aren't there also UNITA members in the batallion?

Belmundo: No, there aren't UNITA members in 32 Batallion. When it was founded, about 3,500 members of the FNLA were integrated into the South African army. Afterwards, South Africa recruited in the refugee camps where there were FNLA and UNITA. The South African officer Liebenberg made use of hunger in the refugee camps, while he provided favorable conditions in the military camps. Angolans were threatened and forced to join UNITA in the bush.

Interviewer: What was the base Pica Pau you mentioned?

Belmundo: The Pica Pau base was for Angolan mercenaries, and for mercenaries from all Western countries.

Interviewer: But they interviewed a UNITA prisoner who had been in the Pica Pau base. Weren't your group and UNITA together there?

Belmundo: UNITA has its base, but it's not the same base as Pica Pau. Pica Pau was for integration of FNLA troops into the South African army. Later they recruited in the refugee camps in Namibia. UNITA and 32 Batallion later also recruited among Angolan workers who had finished their contracts. The total number in 32 Batallion at Pica Pau eventually came to some 9,000 Angolans. [This number is larger than others given for 32 Batallion, and may reflect the total number who passed through the base rather than the total at any one time—ed.] But UNITA didn't have anything to do with this base.

What UNITA did was request that force to cooperate in their zone. Whenever UNITA has a zone they want to occupy, the UNITA leaders contact the South Africans, and the South Africans send troops from the 32 Batallion for an operation in that zone. And afterwards UNITA claims the operation. In fact these are the majority of the operations UNITA claims.

Interviewer: Is that only in Cuando Cubango or in other zones as well?

Belmundo: In all the zones. Whenever the South Africans give the orders.

Interviewer: Trevor Edwards and you both referred to British, Rhodesian, Canadian and other foreign mercenaries in 32 Batallion. Are there also any from other African countries?

Belmundo: No, there are no blacks from other African countries in 32 Batallion. They are in other batallions, such as 31 Batallion, which has about 1,000 Bushmen, some of them Angolans, that functions near the Zambian border. It has Zambians and black Rhodesians as well. Its base is about 70 km from 32 Batallion. Many other Africans—Zimbabweans, Mozambicans—went to train in South Africa. These other Africans you find more often in the special forces, such as Recce Five [Five Reconnaisance Regiment, used after

1980 to lead the Mozambique National Resistance (MNR)—ed.].

Interviewer: In the course you took in South Africa, was there any political training?

Belmundo: The course was a technical military course. We were just prepared for war.

Interviewer: Did you ever see Savimbi?

Belmundo: Savimbi was the favorite son of the South Africans. This is why South Africa gives a lot of aid and protection to Savimbi. I only saw him once in Rundu [northern Namibia], getting out of a Puma helicopter. We were at the base and the helicopter arrived. He was with South African officers and was received immediately by Col. du Plessis, a French mercenary integrated into the South African army. That was the only time I saw Savimbi.

But several times I did see his people such as Lopes—José Lopes Ferreira, a white from Menongue who regularly supplied the UNITA bases at night. The warehouse for logistics for UNITA was right there, and he supplied UNITA with parachutes. Let me tell you a story. One time in South Africa the police captured 400 tons of ivory. In South Africa and Namibia elephant hunting is prohibited. Where did this ivory come from? The investigation reached the conclusion that it came from Namibia and before that from Cuando Cubango, and that it was Savimbi, in collaboration with Col. du Plessis and Lopes, who was responsible. Du Plessis was the South African soldier responsible for northeast Namibia.

Interviewer: Your instructors in Durban, where did they come from?

Belmundo: From all over, southern Africa, French, Americans, Portuguese, from all the Western countries. The largest number were from Israel.

Appendix 2C: Testimony from UNITA Deserters

Note: These testimonies are taken from Angolans who fled UNITA ranks and testified at a tribunal in Luanda, at the beginning of December, 1983. They were videotaped and replayed at hearings in Amsterdam by the Dutch Anti-Apartheid Movement, December 14-18, 1983. The texts below are translated from Karel L. Roskam et al, *Grenzeloze Oorlog: Zuid-Afrika's Agressie Tegen De Buurlanden* (Amsterdam: Uitgeverij Jan Mets, 1984); English translation by William Minter.

Rufino Satumbo

My name is Rufino Satumbo, my *nom de guerre* is Makarof. I am 26 years old and I was born at the Kuando mission station. I have been to 3rd grade and in 1975 I was a worker. I worked on a Portuguese wharf, in Viana. I have no father and my mother was already quite old in 1975; I have not seen her since then.

On February 4, I was 18 then, I became a UNITA soldier. I don't know how. They sent me first to Huambo, then to Bié and finally to Kuando-Kubango. My work was to give permission for soldiers to hunt game. On these trips we went with a car and I had never had military training, but I did have a weapon.

In 1976 we had to go into the forest on foot; we made huts out of branches. There we didn't do much, just hunt for food. We forced people to give us maize to make porridge. Those who refused were killed.

When we went to the villages, sometimes we set fire to them, while the people we knew to sympathize with the MPLA were killed. Sometimes we only went to the villages to steal food.

At our bases there were also civilians, many women and children. The civilians were guarded by the soldiers to prevent them from running away and telling where we could be found.

Most of the women were for the leaders, who picked them out in the villages. They chose girls of 12, 13, 14, and 15 years old; those who didn't come by themselves were tied up. The leaders had many women and often changed them.

The women and children were there against their will. The mothers were always concerned to find food for their babies; many starved of hunger because the nourishment was not good. There was no clinic; there were only traditional doctors. The people who died were not buried, they lay in the corners rotting.

I often thought about running away, but we were watched closely. They also said that those who reported themselves to FAPLA would be killed.

In 1977 or 1978 the FAPLA [Angolan government troops] arrived at the base where we were. I got a bullet in my leg and I was taken to the Chivanda clinic in Namibia. The patients in the clinic were all Angolans and the doctors were South Africans. Afterwards they sent me to a school in Chivanda, where I got military training. The instructors were an Angolan, Eugénio Dala, and three South Africans. I stayed seven months at the clinic. They taught me to set mines on roads. The lesson material came from South Africa, it was written in English. I had six months training and afterwards we waited for some months at Delta base in Namibia. Afterwards, they organized a batallion and we were sent to Angola. At our departure they said, "You should destroy bridges, dams and other things." And they pointed out on the map where we should go.

The leaders of the batallion were Francisco Chinhama and Zé Maria. We first stayed near the Cunene. We attacked villages to sabotage things and steal food. We had instructions to sabotage everything. When we went to attack people in villages, we went alone. When we were going to attack the FAPLA, the South Africans went with us because we couldn't manage that alone. The South Africans had the habit of taking vehicles with them to South Africa, as well as tractors and people's cattle. After the South Africans left our platoon we went further inside the country.

We went first in the direction of Elanda base, but we stayed in the bush. There we did many things. Above all, my specialty, planting mines on the road. The first mine I planted blew up a car with many people, including women and children. We planted the mines at night, at 2 or 3 o'clock, so that people from the villages couldn't see us. After planting the mines we lay in ambush. When a car hit the mine, we killed the people or captured them. We stole the food they had, when we couldn't take any more, we set fire to it. Of the people we captured, the young men stayed with us to become soldiers; the women and children also stayed with us. The somewhat older men were taken to Namibia to go work for the South Africans. The South Africans paid our leaders 2,000 escudos (?) apiece. It was the same in recruiting soldiers. The money stayed with the leaders, it didn't go to the workers who were sold.

We attacked mostly not military vehicles but civilian vehicles, of merchants and of ordinary people and even two times a car full of women and children. They all died. Those were the instructions our leaders gave us. I planted many mines, so many I can't count, and I don't know how many people were killed by them.

I had time and again thought of running away, but I was very scared. When the leaders found out that someone wanted to run away, they took him to Namibia to be punished by the South Africans. They tied up soldiers who wanted to run away and set fire to them. The common people also couldn't run away, they were well guarded to prevent them from reporting where we were.

One day in 1982 a major named Carlos wanted to surrender to the FAPLA. The leaders found him out, tied his legs and took him to Namibia. I was scared to death and then I really decided to run away. On September 28 of that year I turned myself in in Huambo.

Florindo Joaquim Jonatao

My name is Florindo Joaquim Jonatao, I come from Huambo and I am 22 years old.

In 1976 I was only 14 and I was a student in the fourth grade of the Sarmento Rodrigues industrial school. On Saturday, February 8 of that year, I was playing football with seven of my fellow students, when a major of UNITA, named Bantua, appeared and forced us to go with him in a Range-Rover. We didn't know where we were going.

We left Huambo at 4 pm and came on the next day, the 9th, at 6 am to Kuito Kuanavale. A white captain, Perestrelo, came up to us and said that the MIGs of the FAPLA were coming. We set the vehicles we had come in on fire and we went in the forest. In June of July of that year we met colonel N'zau Puna, Chindondo and others, who joined our leaders. During the nights we stayed spread out in the woods. My fellow students and I carried the luggage of the leaders.

Then there began for me and my football friends the way of suffering: a long trip through the wilderness, without shoes, with cold and hunger.

In March 1977 we came to a base where we met Savimbi. At that moment the FAPLA attacked the base and Savimbi fled to South Africa. We followed our leaders. In October Savimbi came back with a batallion of troops, who accompanied an American journalist who came to film an attack of the UNITA troops on FAPLA. The soldiers of the batallion carried new weapons, AKs of Chinese manufacture. This was the first of this kind I had seen. They organized a spectacle, with one half of the troops on one side and the other half on the other side. The two groups shot in the air and those who played the role of the FAPLA fell to the ground, let their weapons fall and acted as if they were dead. And that was the 'battle' that the American journalist filmed. After that they went away and I didn't see Savimbi again.

I continued carrying the baggage through the woods and I suffered a lot. After that, when they had seen that I was intelligent, they let me do the planning of the work.

In 1978 I was separated from my fellow students, of whom two had died of hunger. We were quite weak because we ate only fruit of the trees and bushes. Numerous soldiers tried to run away and to link up with the FAPLA.

In the year 1979 we went to another area, in the Kuanza-Sul province, where major Chissango was the leader. We were with about one hundred men and because we were quite weak, we stayed there to strengthen up. I stayed there six months, and because we had better to eat, cassava and game from hunting, my body developed rapidly. They let me do administrative work for about a year.

On night in April 1981 we were called for roll-call. We grouped ourself in battle formation and began to run without knowing what our destination was. We ran for three days and then we came to the Kangolo plateau, on the border of the Bie, Kuanza-Sul and Huambo provinces. When we had arrived, there also came troops and captured people from other areas. We stayed divided into groups, each with its own task, cut down trees, clearing the grass to make an open space. We didn't eat more than a corn cob a day.

Some days later, on a night in April, the commanders gave us instructions to make fires. Because it was raining, the fire didn't catch and the leaders began to beat us. Then we succeeded in starting the fire. At that moment an airplane appeared and we began to run away. The commanders told us not to run away, because these were our allies and not the enemy. The leaders always spoke of "our allies" and they forbade us to use the words "South Africans" or "Carcamanos." After this reconaissance flight three other airplanes came—it was about midnight—which dropped crates with parachutes.

One of the parachutes didn't open and the crates broke open and the preserves they contained got mixed with explosives which were in other crates. People gathered it up and ate everything, food mixed with explosives. By 6 am there were more than 25 dead from eating the explosives.

The following day we began to transport the material which, among other things, contained: AK-47 weapons of South African manufacture, mines including anti-tank mines, 81- and 82-mm mortars, AK-21 weapons, RPG rockets, other AK weapons of Chinese manufacture, weapons of the FAL type from South Africas, and G-3 weapons made in Portugal.

There were also some uniforms and blankets for the leaders and small boxes of food. All this material was without any marks of the country of origin, so that no one could identify it. But we knew that everything came from South Africa. In August 1981, they called me for a course in communications technology which lasted a month. The instructor was lieutenant Fuma and the material that we used was RACAL-radios from South Africa and England. After the course I trained for six months and afterwards I was placed in the southern sector as a radio operator.

In the reports that we had to give one often spoke of the deaths of FAPLA soldiers. But really it was the civilian population that they killed, because when they came back, they had dishes, washbowls, grain, and household animals with them. They said that these were from the Department of Military Affairs, the results of thefts from the people. Often they put animal blood ont their uniforms so as to say that they had killed FAPLA soldiers.

That was in agreement with the orders of Savimbi in 1980. He had given instructions to all leaders of bases to open a "surprise offensive" against people who refused to work with UNITA. This "surprise offensive" was cutting off of noses, cutting off of breasts, raping women, and above all killing those who didn't accept the UNITA policy.

The night of December 31, 1981, the FAPLA came close to our base. Several of us, mainly women and children, tried to run away and about 6 am on January 1, 1982, I was taken prisoner by FAPLA. They brought me to Catchiungo, afterwards to Huambo and to Bié. They have treated me well. In March 1982 I saw my parents again after seven years separation and now they visit me every week.

In all the years that I was in the bush, I saw no school and I never again played football. All family members of the leaders go for six months each year outside the country for military courses. In all these years I never got clothes, not even a pair of shoes and the sandals that I had on when I was captured were quickly broken by so much walking. I had to walk barefoot, for kilometers with the food of the leaders on my back. They didn't share the food with us and I had to fend for myself. The leaders disliked us, they disliked intelligent children. Some couldn't even write their names, they were just soldiers.

All the time my only concern was to get enough food. Now I want to study, to do a course in agriculture. I didn't have anything all these years, for me it was lost time.

Luciana João Nanga Batista
My name is Luciana João Nanga Batista, I am 16 years old and born in Huambo. My mother's name is Amélia Namala, I

have two brothers and a sister. I haven't seen them for some time. My father is dead. I cannot read or write.

I lived with my mother in Huambo. One day, I was then 10, I went with my friend Joaquina to Bié to visit some friends of ours. The day we came to Cangulo, we sat talking in the house and then we heard shots. When we went outside, we saw that we were surrounded. They were soldiers of UNITA. When they saw us, they picked a number of us. They blindfolded me and took us with them. We didn't know where. With us the soldiers also took many people; men, women, and children were forced to go with them. We travelled several days and came to Mussende. There they let us work; do washing, cook, carry water, and other things. They never let me play. I never again played. We slept in the forest, in the rain and in the cold. The houses were for the leaders and their wives. We were very hungry.

They forced all the women to be naked in order not to escape. One time one of the leaders picked me out to sleep with him and become his wife. I didn't want to because I was still very young, I had not even menstruated yet, I didn't want any man. Moreover, he was very big, strong, and old; he had gray hair.

When I said that I didn't want to, he threatened to beat me. Then I went with him and lived with him in his house. Each time that he made love with me and I didn't want to, he threatened to beat me and he did beat me. Each time I had to go to bed with him.

I didn't have to live outside anymore and I stayed in the house with the leader. I still had to be naked, but I ate better. Apart from having to sleep with him, I worked in the kitchen, did his washing and at night I had to fetch water from the river.

But I could not help it that I felt how my family must think and my husband hit me. I liked nothing about the life there. My husband often went away at night to attack the people. He stayed away several days and when he came back he said: we have taken much food, pigs, chickens, and other things. Who was not with us, we have killed or brought with us. He